Dancing in the World

How can we create more inclusive spaces in the field of dance?

This book presents a framework for dance practitioners and researchers working in diverse dance cultures to navigate academia and the professional dance field. The framework is based on the idea of "cultural confluences," conjuring up an image of bodies of water meeting and flowing into and past one another, migrating through what the authors refer to as the *mainstream* and *non-mainstream*. These streams are fluid categories that are associated with power, privilege, and the ability (or inability) to absorb other cultural forms in shared dance spaces. In reflective interludes and dialogues, Emoghene and Spanos consider the effects of migration on their own individual experiences in dance to understand what it means to carry culture through the body in various spaces. Through an analysis of language, aesthetic values, spaces, creative processes, and archival research practices, the book offers a collaborative model for communicating the value that marginalized dance communities bring to the field.

This book will be of great interest to students, scholars, and arts administrators in dance.

Sinclair Ogaga Emoghene, M.F.A., is a choreographer, dancer, researcher, and assistant professor at Virginia Commonwealth University, Richmond, VA, USA.

Kathleen A. Spanos, Ph.D., is a dancer, educator, and scholar who is a co-founder of the arts non-profit EducArte and assistant director of communications for the University of Maryland Honors College.

Routledge Series in Equity, Diversity, and Inclusion in Theatre and Performance
Series Editor – Brenda Foley

The Equity, Diversity, and Inclusion (EDI) book series is an interdisciplinary forum for exploring diverse identities, concepts, practices, and people in theatre and performance. Through the series, the Theatre and Performance division at Routledge aims to expand its current offerings in response to an overwhelming call to action by participants in the field. The new series reflects both a structure and an ethos, cutting across existing Routledge categories of theatrical production, theatre studies, and research monographs as a means to increase visibility and address the historical exclusion of marginalized voices.

The EDI series' commitment to diversity includes—but also extends beyond—that which we know to be lacking in the field of theatre and performance. We welcome proposals that expand our perspectives and that of the field and look forward to reading your submissions.

Out of Time?
Temporality in Disability Performance
Elena Backhausen, Benjamin Wihstutz, Noa Winter

Dancing Motherhood
Ali Duffy

The Loss of Small White Clouds
Dementia in Contemporary Performance
Morgan Batch

Performing Human Rights
Artistic Interventions into European Asylum
Anika Marschall

For more information about this series, please visit: https://www.routledge.com/Routledge-Series-in-Equity-Diversity-and-Inclusion-in-Theatre-and-Performance/book-series/EDI

Dancing in the World
Revealing Cultural Confluences

Sinclair Ogaga Emoghene
Kathleen A. Spanos

Routledge
Taylor & Francis Group

LONDON AND NEW YORK

First published 2024
by Routledge
4 Park Square, Milton Park, Abingdon, Oxon OX14 4RN

and by Routledge
605 Third Avenue, New York, NY 10158

Routledge is an imprint of the Taylor & Francis Group, an informa business

© 2024 Sinclair Ogaga Emoghene and Kathleen A. Spanos

The right of Sinclair Ogaga Emoghene and Kathleen A. Spanos to be
identified as authors of this work has been asserted in accordance with
sections 77 and 78 of the Copyright, Designs and Patents Act 1988.

British Library Cataloguing-in-Publication Data
A catalogue record for this book is available from the British Library

ISBN: 9781032138114 (hbk)
ISBN: 9781032138756 (pbk)
ISBN: 9781003231226 (ebk)

DOI: 10.4324/9781003231226

Typeset in Times New Roman
by KnowledgeWorks Global Ltd.

Godly Confluence, also known as Devprayag—the place where the Alaknanda and Bhagirathi rivers join to form the Ganga in the state of Uttarakhand, India. Photo credit: Ashwini Chaudhary.

Contents

About the authors

Sinclair Ogaga Emoghene is a dancer and researcher whose work investigates the body as a performance surface while reconstructing the ways that historical data in dance are structured, presented, and archived. His work borders performance creation, place situating, cultural studies, experimental practice, and dance technology. He received his M.F.A. from the University of Maryland, College Park, and is an assistant professor of dance at Virginia Commonwealth University, where he teaches theory, creative research, and dance technique. He has created works for the Nollywood audience in Nigeria/Africa, the John F. Kennedy Center in Washington, D.C., and other prestigious institutions. He is the founder and artistic director of WXYZ Arts Factory and Sinclair Dance.

Kathleen A. Spanos is a dancer, educator, scholar, and arts administrator from the Washington, D.C., area. She is an Irish dancer with a B.A. in cognitive science from the University of Virginia, an M.A. in traditional Irish dance from the University of Limerick, and a Ph.D. in dance and performance studies from the University of Maryland, College Park. Her doctoral work focused on Irish and African cultural influences in masquerades and festivals on the Caribbean island of Montserrat. Kate also completed a postdoctoral Fulbright project on frevo dance in Recife, Brazil. She is a co-founder of EducArte, a 501(c)3 non-profit arts education organization in Maryland.

Acknowledgments

We would like to acknowledge our funders for various aspects of this project, including Virginia Commonwealth University's VCUarts Dean's Faculty Research Grant program, the NextLOOK artist residency program (The Clarice at the University of Maryland and Joe's Movement Emporium), and the Maryland State Arts Council.

We are grateful to the editorial team at Routledge and Taylor & Francis for their support, especially Laura Hussey, Brenda Foley, and Swati Hindwan. We would like to thank our friends and mentors for many clarifying conversations and writing feedback, especially MK Abadoo, Karen Bradley, Crystal Davis, and Kate Sicchio. Special thanks to our editor, Rachel Miller, for her insightful guidance, questions, and attention to detail.

Sinclair acknowledges his colleagues at Virginia Commonwealth University (VCU) who have inspired, encouraged, and guided him throughout this process, including Scott Putnam, Elgie Gaynell Sherrod, Trebien Pollard, Judy Steel, Julian Kevon Glover, Eric Rivera, and Autumn Proctor Waddell, as well as the VCU B.F.A. dance students. Special thanks to VCU leadership, including Courtney Harris, James Wiznerowicz, and Lea Marshall for believing in him and supporting this research journey, and to Carmelita Higginbotham for uplifting his work and promoting underrepresented voices in the School of the Arts. He thanks his mentors in Nigeria, Chris Ugolo and Israel M. Wekpe, for their guidance as he navigates his experience as a migratory dancer in the United States. Thanks to Mustapha Braimah and Momar Ndiaye for their support, brotherhood, and collegiality.

Kate would like to acknowledge Greg Staley and Randy Ontiveros of the University of Maryland's Honors Humanities program for inviting her to design and teach a dance ethnography course that has served as a classroom laboratory for ideas presented in this book. She thanks her teachers and mentors Otávio Bastos, Catherine Foley, and Fabinho Soares, and her dance colleagues, especially Becky Hill and Rebecca McGowan, for many insightful conversations about steps and culture. She is grateful to her family and especially her partner, Pablo Regis de Oliveira, for his support and collaboration, as well as for suggesting that she and Sinclair write this book together.

Introduction

Revealing cultural confluences

Our conversations for this book started when we ran into each other at a samba dance party at a pizza joint in the suburbs of Washington, D.C. The party was organized by Kate and her partner Pablo de Oliveira, a Brazilian musician, for the region's Brazilian music and dance community. Pablo's band played classic samba favorites, and a makeshift dance floor opened up amidst the tables where people were eating and drinking. Folks were dancing and singing along, and at one point the percussionists took over with a carnival-style samba *batucada*, featuring a breakdown of polyrhythms played on drums, shakers, and even knives against plates. Brazilians and non-Brazilians alike jumped out of their seats and shook their hips, their complex footwork dialoguing with the percussion. Dancers formed a *roda*, or circle, into which one or two entered at a time to the excited cheers of onlookers and fellow dancers.

Sinclair happened to arrive at just this moment with some friends who were part of the local Brazilian dance community. He noted a familiar energy in the room. Although the spoken language was different, the rhythmic language of samba and the atmosphere of communal dancing and singing reminded him of his home in Nigeria. We greeted each other with surprise, not expecting to meet each other at this party, and we danced a little samba together. Kate had never witnessed Sinclair's ballroom samba skills, having known him as an African dancer throughout their time in graduate school; and Sinclair had not seen Kate's samba moves, having known her as an American Irish dancer and not knowing much about her ties to D.C.'s Brazilian community. Neither of our sambas looked like the "authentic" samba of the native Brazilians in the room, but no one cared. We both understood the energy of dancing with live music and percussion, with crowds of people sharing a space for cultural expression. We felt comfortable there. We were both somehow outsiders and insiders at the same time, having been invited into the space through our different connections to the community.

That moment sparked a conversation between us about the often-surprising connections that can take shape between dancers as they migrate from one place to another. We became increasingly fascinated by what happens when different kinds of dance are translated and transposed into new contexts. It wasn't just the impromptu samba we danced together at the pizza joint. Other instances of dance worlds colliding quickly sprang to mind, arising from our experiences

DOI: 10.4324/9781003231226-1

with practicing dances outside of their communities of origin, specifically Nigerian dance and Irish dance. We recounted incidents in which we felt out of place and undervalued due to our dance identities, but also times when we felt accepted and at home. We were surprised to find that, despite the differences in our cultural backgrounds, we found a lot of resonance in each other's stories. We realized how much we could learn from each other.

We decided to explore this connection further, and we quickly found that our experiences as dancers working in specific cultural forms have been shaped by preconceptions about us and the dances we practice. Some questions arose: How do dancers practice their cultural traditions outside of their communities of origin? How do we engage with dance cultures outside of our own? We began to discuss how we navigate elements of language, space, sound, and rhythm in our dance forms in the context of academia, where expectations about how to dance are different from those in our own communities. We found that we both care deeply about breaking down barriers to create more equitable access for professional dancers and dance scholars working within forms that have been historically marginalized based on race, ethnicity, or nationality in these spaces. Such barriers include, for example, requiring artists to "translate" the value of their work for gatekeepers; requiring them to use the "right" language to describe what they do; and boxing such artists into the idea of "tradition," not recognizing how their dance forms can also be contemporary and innovative. These conversations led to the conviction that we needed to create a framework together that would reflect our points of connection, as well as our differences, as dancers.

When we talk about diversity and inclusion in the dance field, we refer to the incorporation of more cultural practices and systems into educational curricula and arts programming beyond the forms of ballet and modern dance that predominate Western spaces. This process involves more than just adding, for example, "Black dance" or "African dance" to the curriculum, but it requires a reconfiguration of spaces where dance is expected to take place, as well as the aesthetic systems that we use to evaluate dance. At the core of our writing is an effort to diversify the homogenous categories that are commonly described as, for example, White dance, Black dance, European dance, African dance, Western dance, non-Western dance, and other descriptors that separate dances (and dancers) by race, ethnicity, nationality, or geography. Although these labels provide a general sense of where a dance comes from, we believe that such categories are ultimately limiting for everyone involved and pressure practitioners to "stay in their lane," stifling creativity and cross-cultural expansion. In dance, "colonization through categorization" (as described by Shobana Jeyasingh, qtd. in Chakravorty [2000, 114]) creates a system that does not include dancers who exist outside of or at the intersections of these categories and does not recognize the vast diversity that exists within each category. In addition, such categorization inhibits the migrations and flow that would allow dance cultures around the world to thrive.

In our writing, we aim to reveal how various cultural expressions connect within shared environments and what value we can find in cross-cultural encounters like the one we had at the pizza restaurant. The idea of "revealing cultural confluences" in the title of this book conjures up an image of two rivers meeting. Here, discrete bodies of water pool together at points of *confluence*, forming tributaries that branch off into smaller streams. Similarly, we see dance cultures flowing into and past one another in confluent spaces, joining together, influencing each other, and separating to create new forms. As we describe in more detail in Chapter 1, the framework of cultural confluences that we develop throughout this book is similar to Mary Louise Pratt's notion of "contact zones" in the sense that both describe social spaces where cultures meet and often clash along asymmetrical power relations (1991). *Confluences*, however, also take into account the fluid migration and movement of dancers and their dance cultures through various such spaces. We feel compelled to frame our work around migrations through confluent spaces because bodies and the cultural identities they represent are always moving and adapting to different power dynamics in various contexts.

In framing our work around confluences, we find resonance in anthropologist Eric Wolf's critique of structuralist models that describe the notion of essentialist, fixed cultures running up against each other:

> By turning names into things, we create false models of reality. By endowing nations, societies or cultures, with the qualities of internally homogeneous and externally distinctive bounded objects, we create a model of the world as a global pool hall in which the entities spin off each other like so many hard and round billiard balls. Thus, it becomes easy to sort the world into differently colored balls, to declare that "East is East, and West is West, and never the twain shall meet."
>
> (1982, 6–7)

Dance forms in particular remain permeable and adaptive to cultural influences in their proximity because of the ways that bodies migrate throughout spaces, as we describe throughout this book. But we note that some are less permeable than others, either because of their dominance in the space or due to standards set up to protect, preserve, or control them. The shape of a dance culture may be upheld internally by community leaders and tradition bearers, but it may also be controlled by outsiders who place borders around it and tell practitioners what their culture is and should be. As we discuss throughout this book, colonization has profoundly shaped global communities in ways that require us, as dancers, to consider how we inhabit the categories that we have been placed in and how we can push out of them.

We hear a lot of conversations in the dance field today about fluidity and nuance, but we do not always see these values in practice, especially when funding, access to resources, or reputation is at stake. And when leaning too far into the metaphor of fluidity and universality, these conversations sometimes ignore the nuances of cultural specificity as they reinforce the utopian mantra, "dance is for everyone." Dance *is* for everyone, but we must first clarify how dance does not mean the same thing to everyone.

Thus, "Dancing in the World: Revealing Cultural Confluences" aims to reimagine dance spaces in academia and the professional dance field in order to recognize marginalized dance communities that are often barred from inclusion and legitimization in a global context. Our work challenges systems of privilege and hierarchy, proposes more inclusive structures, and makes space for dancers from all communities to work on their own terms. In research, the reconfiguration we call for means challenging power hierarchies such as those between theory and practice or academic and non-academic communities, and throughout this book, we focus especially on power relations at the intersections of race, ethnicity, and nationality. We consider the ways that artists from so many dance cultures around the world have been excluded from what are considered dances of "value" in economic terms and what these cultures offer the dance field at large. One of our aims in this book is to propose factors for determining the value of a dance culture beyond its economic potential in the global marketplace. That is, we want to establish methods for describing the value that is generated through dance within local communities. The energy that is shared among people dancing together is difficult to describe in words, but it is felt in the body. We look toward approaches to teaching, performance, and research in dance that emphasize cultural appreciation, process-oriented work, and continual questioning, as well as approaches that challenge biases and assumptions; expand aesthetic definitions of what is considered "good" in dance; and recognize the power of embodied knowledge arising from culturally specific epistemologies.

We are especially interested in dances that are not performed to be "consumed" or performed on the concert stage or in a studio, but rather are to be shared and experienced in homes and kitchens, in ritual spaces, on the streets, in dance clubs, or in other community spaces. What can we learn from the systems and structures that communities already use to organize themselves, present, and participate in their own dance events? Are the artists who are creating within these "unconventional" spaces getting the recognition and support they need to keep doing their work? Or are they being discouraged? In what ways does being in an unwelcoming, unfamiliar, or inappropriate environment, without the cultural cues necessary to complete a dance ritual, hinder both the preservation of tradition as well as innovation? How can we replace the concept of discrete, parallel, and restrictive "lanes" with one of confluent streams to create spaces that encourage more generative collaboration across these boundaries?

Migrations and cultural confluences

We are writing this book together because, despite our different backgrounds and experiences, we have discovered through our conversations a shared perspective on what is missing in the dance field in the United States today and how we might contribute to diversifying perspectives on how dance creates meaning and value for people. We both have extensive experience with dances in various parts of the world, but this book focuses primarily on how dance cultures are represented in the United States, where both of us currently live and work. We both see ourselves as "migratory dancers" who have moved across geographical borders and through various cultural spaces as artists and scholars. We also recognize that, by virtue of being academics in the United States, we have a certain amount of power and privilege, even if the dance forms we practice are outside of the mainstream in the context of dance academia.

By way of introduction, Sinclair Ogaga Emoghene draws from his experience growing up within the collection of seven large cultural groupings in Delta State, Nigeria: the Orua Ivie Abraka Kingdom, which includes Ero (his mother's village) and Uro Ivie (his father's village). In these communities, dance is used as a way of understanding, celebrating, and activating knowledge about the region's cultural history and traditions while also appreciating these cultural touchstones. *Udje* dances and songs, which are performed at festivals to establish and maintain social norms, were the earliest forms he learned (see Ojaide 2001). His own family hosted such performances when he was young. Growing up in the 1980s and 1990s, his family also traveled across Nigeria and England, which exposed him to Western culture. In Nigeria, they settled in Jos, Plateau State, which served as a melting pot for various cultures in the country's Middle Belt area. His family spoke Urhobo as their native tongue and Nigerian pidgin English. During his early years, he also learned various languages like Hausa, the predominant northern language; Igbo from his Igbo neighbors; and Ukwale.

It was at the tertiary level of his education, at the Federal University of Benin (Uniben) in Edo State, that Sinclair began formally studying theatre and dance history. During his time at Uniben, he interacted with and learned from the Benin dance theatre at the Oba Akenzua Cultural Center, which is closely tied to the Oba (king) of Benin palace of the Ancient Benin Empire. As he learned Edo's rich cultural songs, dance, and dramaturgy, it became clear to him that his people of Orua Ivie (a system comprising seven clans) in Abraka, Delta State shared a close relationship and lineage. He began to identify how his worldview and cultural sensitivities stem from the cultural history of his people and the Binis (people from Benin City in Edo State). This experience led him to various research endeavors about dance histories, forms, and styles that he now shares in his dance career as a teacher, choreographer, theorist, and dancer in the United States. He has lived in the United States since 2013 when he arrived to complete a Master of Fine Arts degree at the University of Maryland, and he is now an assistant professor of dance at Virginia Commonwealth University. Acknowledging the multidimensional facets of his lineage as a dancer, he seeks to understand dance cultures from a place of curiosity, appreciation, and sharing.

Kate Spanos is a dancer and dance scholar who draws from her experience growing up in the United States in a family of Irish and Greek heritage. She started dancing as a child at Irish *céilís* (social gatherings) and trained in competitive Irish step dance in northern Virginia, just outside of Washington, D.C., and central Virginia until she graduated from college. She was raised with a strong sense of connection to both Irish and Greek cultures, including language, customs, and religion. Dance and music came to the forefront of her experience at a young age, living in the United States and making frequent visits to Greece and Ireland.

After graduating from the University of Virginia with a degree in cognitive science and computer science, she studied in Ireland, where she completed a Master's in traditional Irish dance at the University of Limerick. There she was introduced to the vast array of dances that comprise the category of "traditional Irish dance," ranging from step dancing in counties Cork and Kerry in the southwest to *sean nós* ("old style") dancing in the Connemara region on the west coast and festival style dancing in Northern Ireland. Studying in Ireland taught her, an Irish American who did not grow up there, that a range of different dance forms exists within this small island nation that, in the diasporic experience, can appear to be a homogeneous culture. Specifically, she learned how dance and music culture was divided and controlled by religious and political boundaries due to British colonization of Ireland over centuries, and she also gained insight into how being an American whose family immigrated to the United States impacts her experience of Irish dance culture.

Kate also studied in the Caribbean, where she conducted doctoral research on the masquerade dances of Montserrat, a British Overseas Territory located in the Leeward Islands. Throughout her research, she studied the island's unique blending of African and Irish cultural influences dating back to the era of the transatlantic slave trade and indentured servitude. In this work, she experienced the interweaving of racial and cultural identities that challenged her preconceptions about categories of "White, "Black," "Irish" or "European," "African," and "Caribbean," or "local" and "non-local." In 2018, her postdoctoral research in Brazil focused on frevo carnival dance in Recife and Olinda in the northeastern state of Pernambuco and its origins in capoeira, which she had practiced since 2008. This project examined embodied strategies of resistance in Brazilian cultural practices to Westernization, elitism, and racism. With a strong sense of her cultural background as an American Irish dancer, her ethnographic experiences have taught her how to cultivate curiosity about people and their cultures and how to develop better questions to understand the embodied elements that bring value to their dance forms.

As we discuss throughout this book, much of the problem with how our dance cultures are received and perceived in the United States relates to issues of migration and diaspora—being uprooted from a home culture and transposed to a new one. As dancers of non-dominant forms, both of us have struggled to express what we value about our forms in academic settings. We have felt policed through language and terminology, pedagogical expectations, and other institutionalized practices meant to ensure the preservation of "tradition" and "authenticity." In this framework, we see migration as distinct from just visiting or passing through, which may result in simply feeling out of place or unfamiliar like a tourist but not alienated or "Othered," as is often the case for someone trying to create a stable life in a new environment. In addition, migration is about more than moving from point A to point B but, rather, involves a complex web of exchange and power dynamics. As we describe through examples in the following chapters, both of us have felt like we are "nowhere" or without a foundation to stand on as we migrate through various spaces. Such migrations include the experience of physically moving from one geographical location to another (as in Sinclair immigrating to the

United States), as well as the experience of practicing a cultural dance form outside of the mainstream within a particular geographical location (as in Kate learning Irish dance in the United States, where Irish dance is not as widely practiced as forms like ballet, jazz, or modern). We feel confronted with our "Otherness" when outside of our dance communities and, in academia, we feel pressured to explain the dance cultures we come from and translate them for outsiders' comprehension and comfort. We have also felt compelled to "edit" our cultures to please and entertain audiences when creating work for the classroom or the stage—and by "edit," we do not simply mean the minor revisions that all artists and scholars must do to communicate their work, but the blatant omission and silencing of crucial aspects of our cultures because they are too difficult to translate for academic or other outside audiences. The inability to fully express intellectually and creatively inhibits artistic growth, and we have both felt stymied by it.

On the other hand, we have also experienced pressure from members of our own communities to remain true to the culture by operating within frameworks that are considered "traditional" to our forms. We must clarify that, as dancers from specific traditional cultures, we are not against tradition, nor are we against innovation. Instead, as we explain throughout this book, we are concerned with the idea that tradition cannot change, as well as the dangers of detaching the individual from the community—and movements and gestures from a ritual or tradition—when presenting dance outside of its original context, perhaps on a concert stage or in a space designed for another form. Our attempts to develop an artistic voice and expand the boundaries of tradition and innovation are, it seems, met with resistance on all sides. Purists or traditionalists may criticize the artist for not showing respect for the roots or history of a dance, and outsiders may complain that they do not understand the work because it is too "foreign" and does not present the usual, stereotypical markings that make such work legible to those without deep cultural knowledge of the dance. So, too, many dance critics and gatekeepers contend that a dance is not "meaningful" when cultural codes embedded within the dance do not follow familiar modes of storytelling or meaning making, or are not sufficiently translated for outsiders, as we describe in Chapter 4. We want to highlight the cultural specificity of a dancer's kinesthetic experiences in any style while also emphasizing the importance of understanding the communities in which those experiences are rooted.

To that end, migratory dancers like us must be able to explain the specific value that our forms bring to confluent spaces. We entered academia as dancers because we saw an opportunity to take advantage of resources that would support us in researching our forms. We both feel privileged to be in academic spaces while also feeling disadvantaged because of the forms we practice, study, and promote. Our goal is not to offer solutions to address every inequity but to invite people to relate to us and work together toward more equitable solutions to these many varied misunderstandings. There are many case studies about specific dance cultures that brilliantly articulate the value of specific dance communities, but we want to see more work that grapples with the language and frameworks that are used to talk about such dance cultures in U.S. academia on a broader level. This book deals with the effects of migration in dance from various perspectives including the translations of language and aesthetics required to express a form's cultural value (Chapters 1, 2, and 4); the transpositions required to present dance in new spaces (Chapter 3); and the movement and transmission of cultural knowledge through dancing bodies across time and space (Chapter 5). It should not be incumbent on all artists to translate their work for outsiders, but it is a challenge that we embrace in our own efforts as dance scholars to bridge cross-cultural confluent spaces.

Mainstream and non-mainstream in dance

When Sinclair arrived in the United States from Nigeria to start a graduate dance program, he was surprised and confused when, on the first day, he was asked to teach "African dance" to undergraduate students. "What is African dance?" he asked the program director. He had a lifetime of experience with the cultural rituals of his Hausa, Tiv, and Urhobo communities in Nigeria, but he was not sure what to make of this broad category called "African dance," which, to his understanding, spanned an entire continent. How was he to teach all of African dance in one semester? What type of African dance does this label refer to? Was he an African dancer? He learned that "African dance" in the United States usually refers to a high-energy, virtuosic style that is featured in various dances and rhythms from Senegal, Mali, and Guinea. This style is different from Nigerian body stylizations and, more importantly, these movements were not necessarily the first ones Sinclair would draw upon to teach the dance rituals of his home community. Still, he was expected to not only know these forms but also teach them by virtue of being African. He realized that he represented diversity for the program but did not feel he could fulfill expectations of what that diversity should bring to the classroom. This begs the question: Does promoting diversity in dance mean including only what is already part of the conventions that American and European audiences designate as "African dance" (or Indian dance, Mexican dance, Chinese dance, Irish dance, etc.)? Or can "diversity" also include expanding conventional ideas about what these broad categories encompass?

To use monolithic categories like African dance, or other "world," "traditional," or "ethnic" dance terms, means treating a variety of diverse, fluid cultural dance practices as relics of a single, static culture. Once a narrative about a dance label is constructed and circulated, it is difficult to undo. This creates pressure for a dancer to fulfill the expectations of the label and to present the same thing over and over again without the agency to be creative or use the dance form to be more socially aware or politically informed, or engage in intellectual conversations with other dancers. In Sinclair's case, he was expected to know what African dance meant and to present a version of African dance knowledge that Americans were familiar with and comfortable with.

Sometimes we wonder, what could we do with these dance forms if they did not come with preconceived cultural assumptions but instead were treated as "neutral" or "acultural," providing a blank slate for abstract human expression? As Homi Bhabha writes, once an identity has been minoritized or marginalized, that identity exists "somewhere between the too visible and the not visible." That is, these cultural identities are marked and also pushed out of sight. The solution, he says, does not involve "returning to an 'unmarked' authentic origin or pre-text," but must negotiate the "dangerous indeterminacy" caused by this marking (2011, 56). Culture is what we believe makes all dances so valuable and distinct. Thus, achieving neutrality is not our goal, and we believe that there is power in negotiating the uncertainties and tensions that we find along cultural boundaries in confluent spaces. In a globalized world filled with cultural differences, we do not ask that our dance cultures become unmarked, but that they receive equitable treatment in the field without becoming diluted.

As we enter these discussions, terminology is of utmost importance. It is also nearly impossible to get right. In Chapter 1, we delve deeper into the use of language in dance, but it is important to clarify some choices in terminology from the start. Throughout this book, we generally avoid using terms like cultural dance, folk dance, traditional dance, ethnic dance, national dance, ritual dance, or vernacular dance, unless we clarify why we believe a particular term is relevant to the conversation (as in the case of "traditional dance" in Chapter 4). As Joann Kealiinohomoku discusses in her seminal essay, "Folk Dance" (1972), and as countless other dance scholars have discussed, these terms have all been historically wrapped up in conflicting value judgments, biases, and assumptions. We prefer to refer to "dance cultures" to highlight the fact that all dances are part of a particular cultural context. Whereas terms like "world dance" or "cultural dance" focus on the word "dance" and label it with a qualifier like "cultural" or "ethnic" to set it apart from other dances that are not considered "cultural" or "ethnic," we focus on the fact that all dances arise from specific cultural origins, even dominant cultures that may not be clearly marked or visible. Movement itself is meaningless without understanding how it relates to a community's worldview and to the other customs and practices that accompany the dance. Although this line of thinking might also encourage us to remove the word "dance" altogether and just refer to "cultures," especially considering those cultures that do not separate dance from other rituals, traditions, and practices, we hold onto "dance" here in order to clarify our overarching focus on movement and the body.

We draw on the way Marta Savigliano grapples with the term "world dance" as an "aestheticized biopolitics" that is wrapped up in questions of privilege, legitimization, consumption, and ethics (2009). Like world music, world dance is a catch-all category created for the purposes of buying and selling a commodity. It is not an identity embraced by actual dancers. For example, neither of us would ever identify as "world dancers," although the forms we practice are often described as such by outsiders. In the experiences that we relate throughout this book, we describe how, outside of our own dance communities, we are usually only welcome to teach or present work within the category of "world dance," "global dance," or "ethnic dance," whereas "real" dancers are free to work within the broad, unmarked "dance" category. We have both felt the pressure to fit in and be accepted by the concert dance world and to show our "skill" as choreographers and educators within the realm of dance education by altering our aesthetic choices, pedagogical approaches, and creative processes to fit the mold. Savigliano also talks about the separation between "art" or "aesthetic" dance and "anthropological" dance. The former focuses on "presentational" movement practices and the latter has been used as a category for collecting dances into a monolithic archive of the "Other" (2009, 170–174). This sense that the dances we practice are only good for "collecting" or preserving culture is part of what makes us feel excluded and creatively stifled. We may even doubt that we are artists, despite devoting our lives to our dance practices. We address this issue directly in Chapters 4 and 5 when we discuss the challenges of creating new work within a dance tradition and holding embodied knowledge in cultural memory.

Savigliano comments on the Foucauldian ways that, in so-called "world dance," bodies are "disciplined" and "saved" through the imposition of Western performance standards—including choreography, pedagogical standardization, competition, and virtuosity—on dance traditions that are built on improvisation, oral and kinesthetic transmission, and community. For her, the concept of world dance deals "irresponsibly and unaccountably…with displacements of identities onto bodily movements severed from subjectivities" (2009, 178). We know that cultural exchange and cross-pollination between various dance cultures occur as a result of globalization and commodification. Both of us have benefitted from these processes as dancers who have traveled away from home to further our dance careers—Sinclair from Nigeria to study, teach, and create in higher education in the United States; and Kate from the United States to study dance cultures in Ireland, Brazil, and Montserrat. But we also recognize the deleterious effects of having to treat dance cultures as commodities for sale in a competitive global market. We are interested in how aesthetic value systems about what is "good" or "bad" in dance are shaped around these migratory flows (Chapter 2), as well as the effects of displacement, translation, and transposition on dance cultures as they stream through various spaces over time (Chapter 3). Can the value of what we do be described in the same language that is used to commodify and capitalize on dance, or do we need new language to have different kinds of conversations?

Revealing cultural confluences in dance is not just about idly watching forms flow in and out of each other's spheres of influence, but it is about critically determining how power structures regulate the size of these streams, how these streams interact with one another, and which ones gain or lose dominance through these confluences. We approach our examination of the power dynamics between dance cultures using the categories "mainstream" and "non-mainstream" in order to describe the position of a particular dance within any given social system in relation to others. We broadly define mainstream dances as those that receive more funding, resources, and public support than non-mainstream dances in the same pool. In the U.S. academic system, we consider mainstream dance to include ballet and modern, postmodern, and contemporary dance because these are the forms that one generally finds on a concert stage or in a classroom of higher education in this country. We must clarify that we do not have a problem with these dance forms themselves, but with the system that privileges them over others. In our work, both of us have run up against the belief that any type of dance that is not one of these forms does not belong in certain spaces, such as on stages and classrooms in academic institutions, performance venues, and other organizations that distribute resources to dance artists.

The notion of mainstream and non-mainstream suggests a strict binary that goes directly against our invocation of free-flowing confluences. This dissonance is precisely the jarring experience that we have had as dancers who have felt outside of the mainstream and have been told to stay within the bounds of our own dance cultures. We think of mainstream and non-mainstream as streams that cross and intersect kaleidoscopically through the cultural confluences that we describe throughout this book. We align this framing with Stuart Hall's notion of cultural identity not as essentialist but as "a meeting point" and as "strategic and positional" (2011, 3–5), resisting colonization through categorization. Considering the ways that dancers enter and exit the mainstream in different spaces allows us to examine the complexity that exists within and across geographical, cultural, ethnic, national, and racial categories, many of which seem to be at the center of our field's challenges with equity and inclusion.

Another way to talk about mainstream dance is in terms of the privileges that arise from adopting certain aesthetic value systems within a dance culture. Privilege is often discussed in racial terms, and while we fully acknowledge the existence of White privilege, we also want to consider how aesthetic value in dance is privileged by factors beyond and/or in interaction with skin color. In dance, skin color and physical features are put on full display. The dancing body becomes the target of all kinds of commentary, assumptions, and implicit and explicit bias (Davis 2022). When we look at confluences of people and communities in dance, almost no one falls squarely in any one category. As we discuss in Chapter 3, saying that one type of aesthetic is "White" or "Black," "European" or "African," or "Western" or "non-Western" is a limiting framework that pressures people to adopt the aesthetic that is "correct" for their particular identity, and then scolds them for not meeting the expectations that are based on their skin color, even though what is "correct" is unclear. For example, light-skinned samba dancers may identify (or be identified) as White in Brazil but find that they are Brown in the United States. Or a Black dancer from the United States visiting Ghana may be identified as more American than African, and may even be called "White" through their association with the United States. It is a challenge for dancers to adapt to new spaces and the expectations that those spaces demand of them. The Western vs. non-Western distinction is particularly difficult because geographical location does not fully describe the experience of dancers who migrate between cultural environments—as in the case of Sinclair coming from a non-Western country to work in Western academia and share non-Western cultural knowledge; or Kate growing up in a Western country and dancing a non-mainstream Western form (Irish dance) while also going on to study non-Western forms. Such dichotomies arise from colonization and the need to categorize what we do, and we have both experienced limitations as well as privileges based on these expectations as we have passed in and out of the mainstream in various situations throughout our lives.

Our concept of confluent streams expands on the theory of intersectionality, or how the compounding and overlapping of identities arising from an individual's race, gender, class, etc. contribute to experiences of oppression, discrimination, or disadvantage (Crenshaw 1989). How these identities affect one's experience depends on how social categories are defined and privileged (or not privileged) in different parts of the world. We believe that dance provides a vehicle for intersectional human beings to encounter and move with one another in shared confluent spaces. Here we are primarily concerned with those moments of interaction. Our understanding of intersectionality is that an individual is made aware of how their various identities are "activated" by external social forces that then shape their experience. By contrast, we see a confluence as the situation, event, or encounter that brings together people who have those intersectional identities. For example, at the samba party that we describe in this book's opening, we behaved not only according to our intersectional identities in terms of race, gender, class, ethnicity, sexuality, and nationality but also according to the cultural dance knowledge that we carried in our bodies. Sinclair brought his knowledge of ballroom samba, as well as his understanding of social dance events in general. He recalled to Kate, "I remember when I asked you to dance, I nervously told you I had never danced Brazilian samba like this before, but I could only do ballroom samba. You replied that it wasn't a problem—that we could just dance." The two of us started doing some basic steps and Sinclair added some ballroom steps like whisks, botafogos, and turning volta steps. Kate had never done these before but was able to follow. At this moment, we were not thinking about our intersectional identities. We worked together to negotiate what was going on in a space where both of us were outsiders, drawing on and sharing the cultural dance knowledge we held in our bodies. Examining confluent spaces means understanding how our behavior in a particular situation arises not only from being aware of our intersectional identities but also from the subconscious, embodied cultural knowledge that we have about how to negotiate that situation together.

Talking about culture in terms of streams and confluences also considers the ways that dance cultures influence each other. Sometimes influence may be organic; at other times, influence may be considered forceful appropriation or marginalization of one culture by another. We see how mainstream individuals and organizations draw clear boundaries to protect their dance territories, and, as such, they are able to "invite" others to come in and participate. This comes with the assumption and expectation that all dancers and dances can thrive in their mainstream spaces, but the mainstream center still maintains control over resources. In addition, it is common for mainstream forms to both intentionally and unintentionally absorb elements (motifs, rhythms, steps, gestures, etc.) from 'non-mainstream forms and include them in their own. To survive in this environment and maintain their practices under unstable circumstances, dancers who practice non-mainstream forms must be versatile and malleable. But they must also stay on guard.

We recognize that some judgment may be implied by the word "mainstream." Although we use "mainstream" in this book to simply refer to dances that receive more resources and support in particular contexts, some may associate the word with pop culture or giant multimedia corporations in a derogatory way, denoting something that is less "authentic." This negative association is not our intention. As dancers who feel outside of mainstream dance in the United States, we desire to be part of the mainstream in the sense of receiving resources, but not so much that we lose our connection to our communities and become "owned" by a funder, corporation, or institution, compromising our freedom to create on our own terms. Within the capitalist, competitive, and globalized world that we find ourselves in, we are not convinced that the field can achieve full equity and equal sharing of resources. But we do believe that the idea of mainstream and non-mainstream can help us think about how a dance is valued (or not) in various spaces.

In our view, mainstream and non-mainstream are not fixed categories. These terms are not meant to gloss over the messiness of cultural influence and migration, but rather, to lean into it. The idea of flowing in and out of the mainstream also reflects the ways that, within a larger dance culture and even some smaller ones, some practitioners or communities are more valued than others. That is, they receive more funding and public support than other groups in the same pool. The sense that some groups are more dominant than others creates rivalry and competition within the genre, which can be both healthy for and detrimental to a dance culture's growth. The scale tips in and out of favor for some, depending on geography, population, time period, and various social, cultural, and racial considerations. As we describe in Chapter 1, the idea of a dance genre being "mainstream," then, is relative to its sociocultural context and also to the perspective of an individual at any given time. By invoking this framework of cultural confluences, we are opening up a space for dialogue and debate about what mainstream and non-mainstream mean to dancers from different backgrounds and in different situations.

While it is difficult to define all that is needed to achieve systemic change on a broader societal level, our aim in this book is to present the value that non-mainstream dances bring to our understanding of dance in a global context and to optimistically share our vision for what that change could look like. We envision a world in which dance spaces can be configured beyond solely racial, ethnic, national, or geographic boundaries while recognizing, respecting, and celebrating the cultural specificity that arises from those categories. This is neither a call for multiculturalism nor for color blindness, which Brandi Wilkins Catanese explains as the erasure of race through cultural assimilation and the ensuing normalization of Whiteness, on the one hand, and a sort of social amnesia about the effects of racism throughout history, on the other (2011, 3–9). We believe that expanding our definitions of dance beyond limited and limiting binary categories based on race, ethnicity, and geography (White vs. Black, European vs. African, Western vs. non-Western) will benefit all involved. At times throughout this book, we use these general categories for the purposes of explanation, because we recognize that this is common language that is currently used. However, we continually seek to challenge the use of these terms as generalized descriptors. If we must use categories to organize our field, then we propose at least promoting systems that allow for more nuance, confluence, and complexity, rather than relying on simplistic heuristics to make judgments about what is valuable or not. Just as "Black dance" and "African dance" are not one thing, neither are "White dance" or "European dance"; and "Western dance" and dances of the "Global North" are just as diversified, geographically speaking, as "non-Western dance" or dances of the "Global South." We want to see not only a wider representation of faces, bodies, and skin colors in the dance field but an even wider representation of movement practices and aesthetic value systems, as well as spaces where this movement can happen.

As we develop our argument about the need to diversify attitudes about dance, we acknowledge that experiences of exclusion and marginalization are not only limited to dancers of color in Eurocentric spaces. We are careful to not center the experiences of White dancers because we recognize how dancers of color experience vile racism inside and outside of dance spaces. We want to challenge and recalibrate facile definitions promoted by systems of oppression that separate dance forms into discrete, binary categories based on race and ethnicity. We recognize the material impacts of exclusion and delegitimization for dancers of color and the privilege of White dancers in the field. Without diminishing the privilege that White dancers possess due to their skin color, we also believe it is important to point out that White dancers who practice European forms from outside of the U.S. dance field's mainstream, like Kate as an American Irish dancer, have also been excluded and misunderstood. Both of us have felt paralyzed by the oppositional pull of tradition and innovation, finding it difficult to create new work that is both personally expressive and respectful of tradition. We have observed an emphasis on high-energy, virtuosic styles in our respective forms and, as we describe in Chapter 4, we have felt pressured to present something more "professional" or "artistic" on stage. Responding to this pressure requires a process that detaches the tradition from its original context and repurposes it for the concert stage. Our desire to attend to how White dancers also struggle with being misunderstood is part of our effort to recognize how all communities suffer when only one or a few mainstream aesthetics and artistic processes are valued, promoted, and legitimized.

In addition, where there are calls to diversify "Eurocentric dance education," we want to point out that "Eurocentric" generally does not mean education about all dances of European origin, but instead refers specifically to an education based in ballet and/or Western modern dance training. Educating dance students about the aesthetic diversity that exists within predominantly White, European dance cultures is a powerful tool for building empathy and recognizing that no one dance culture or social group is neutral or acultural. In addition, modern dance and Western dance education in the United States have not just been constructed by White European Americans, as we know, but also by African Americans, Latin Americans, and Indigenous artists. Much work has been and is currently being done to recuperate those essential contributions by people and communities of color to our field. To diversify Eurocentric dance education means to not accept just one way of being a "trained" or "intellectual" dancer, but to uplift, influence, and value many other embodied cultural epistemologies in our academic system. In doing so, we will further encourage the development of these forms and expand the creative opportunities for dancers working within them.

In the classroom

Why should the stories of a wider variety of dance cultures be told in classrooms of higher education? Wouldn't these stories be more effectively and tradition- ally taught through firsthand experience in their communities of origin? Do these dances even belong in the studio or classroom? Or are they best learned with sand under the feet, on the warped wood of a rural dance hall, or on a street corner, sur- rounded by family and friends? These are questions that we often hear, and that we ourselves struggle with. To answer them, a good starting point is to ask: What is the purpose of dance education?

In our classes, we encourage students to recognize that, in the realm of dance and culture, the goal is not to collect irrefutable, objective facts, but, rather, to un- derstand that dance research is often subjective, guided by the confluent streams that shape the narratives we tell about ourselves and our communities. As one of Kate's students commented at the end of a semester in her dance ethnography class, "I no longer view styles of dance as intransigent categories but as products of differential experiences unified by collective human embodied knowledge." This comment arose from the student grappling with contradictions between what was written about a dance culture's history; what they saw, heard, and felt in move- ment classes; and what they discussed in an interview with a respected community leader. The student came to understand that the goal of the project was not to be- come an authority on the form but to continually ask better questions. As educators, we can use dance to teach students (and remind ourselves) to recognize what we do not know for sure and continually challenge ourselves intellectually and physically.

The point of teaching about more dance cultures in the classroom is not neces- sarily to train students to become masters in a dance form (unless an extensive multi-level curriculum is developed for that form, which is currently uncommon for non-mainstream dances), but, rather, to give them new experiences that open new possibilities for embodied expression. A ballet student, for example, may have never dropped the pelvis to feel that pull toward the earth, just as a hip-hop dancer may not be used to pulling up through the torso toward the sky, just as an Afrobeats dancer may have never trained a Hortonesque "lateral T," just as an Irish dancer may have never whined their waist. All are beautiful ways of experiencing one's body. As dance educators, both of us aim to equip our students with a toolbox for cultivating curiosity, so that when they, for example, stumble across captivating 15-second videos of Native American hoop dance on TikTok, they do not just scroll past absentmindedly. Instead, a barrage of questions should come to mind. Where does this dance come from? Who dances it? What does it take to move the body like that? Is there a spiritual meaning behind these movements and what the dancers are wearing? How can I learn more about this dance and the people who dance it?

In our teaching, we emphasize the importance of asking students to step into another person's shoes, so to speak, and feel what it feels like to move in ways that are unfamiliar or uncomfortable. This approach requires a consideration of how all students, regardless of their background, can benefit from an introduction to the breadth of cultural expressions that are manifested through physical movement across racial, ethnic, and national boundaries. It is not enough to leave students from any form or cultural background to experiment within the confines of what they already know and feel comfortable with. Learning requires discomfort—both physical and mental. This experience is much like traveling to other parts of the world to gain new perspectives but through body movement. Educators need to develop cultural competency to guide students through the experience of kinesthetic "culture shock" and cultural misunderstandings, in order to reflect on what feels unfamiliar and why. We also need to guide students to recognize that one's own individual movement expression does not exist in a vacuum. The ways we move arise from our cultures and communities.

In this book, we also discuss how these issues play out beyond the classroom in the realm of performance venues and cultural institutions in the professional dance world. How do we build and maintain spaces for dance artists to create and share their work on their own terms? What determines "value" for audiences, and how are dances packaged for them? We are interested in how performance is also educational, not in a didactic manner, but through more participatory, community-based work that can invite audiences to access culture in intimate, embodied ways. Not everyone will understand the nuances of every gesture, but part of the responsibility of the artist is to make creative choices that guide audiences through an experience, much like an educator. What knowledge is embedded in these forms, and how can performers communicate that knowledge to audiences with varying levels of cultural competency in the form? How can we harness the power of "multivocality" in dance work to communicate with diverse audiences? We think it is important to allow room for artists to grow in their own forms. They can avoid exoticization and becoming limited by a "single story" (Adichie 2009) while also making the work accessible to outsiders in ethically responsible ways.

We propose valuing community-based dances as they are, avoiding the pressures to "refine" or "concertize" movement from its communal context for stage presentation, translating contextual meaning for outside audiences. We invite dancers from all backgrounds to cultivate curiosity about other dance forms by offering some examples of the sorts of questions that one might consider when learning about a new dance culture. We do not seek to accomplish the impossible task of eliminating biases and assumptions completely. Instead, we hope to encourage students, dancers, and audiences alike to recognize when those biases arise, identify what they are, question them, and challenge them. It is easy to judge dance based on a single, hegemonic aesthetic system, but how can we be open to new definitions of what constitutes art and beauty? This is an enormous philosophical undertaking, but we think that starting with people and the communities to which they belong offers great insight into how others shape their worlds so that we can expand our own.

Methodologies

Throughout this book, we relate our experiences through vignettes and anecdotes to describe how we have navigated dance spaces up to this point in our relatively young lives. As professional dance artists and scholars working in the United States whose foundational movement training comes from particular dance cultures and not ballet or modern dance, our approach is largely shaped by critical ethnography methods, which D. Soyini Madison defines as "multidisciplinary yet distinctive, open-ended yet precise, contingent yet resilient" (2020, 4). Many of the experiences we present here do not arise from formalized research, but from digging into our memories to reflect on and analyze our lived experiences. Through this work, we locate theory "on the ground" and "in the body" or "in the flesh," drawing on Dwight D. Conquergood's approach to performance, ethnography, and praxis (2013). Through this process of reflection, we realized how much dance had already taught us about how to look at and relate to the world before we even knew to call it research. This work is also semi-autoethnographic. As educational anthropologist Heewon Chang explains, the autoethnographic method arises from the idea that culture is neither solely based in the individual nor in the community, but it is located somewhere in between the "egocentric" and the "sociocentric" (2008, 15–29). We strive to bring our communities into our writing, just as we have struggled to bridge the gap between dance in academia and dance as it is practiced in our cultural communities. Through our reflective interludes and dialogues in this book, we consider the effects of confluence on our own individual experiences to better understand the dynamics of our danced cultural encounters and what it means to carry a culture through dance in various spaces.

We acknowledge that the experiences and anecdotes we share are necessarily limited. Nevertheless, they are still valuable, just as the experience and perspective of every individual are meaningful and carry weight in anthropological work. As historian Luise White demonstrates with her unique historiographical approach in *Speaking with Vampires* (2000), anecdotes and community mumblings can be treated as valid research evidence because even in their contradictions—or *especially* in their contradictions—storytelling and anecdotal knowledge reveal a great deal about people, their communities, and their cultural and social values. As we explain further in Chapter 5, we recognize that our stories do not arise out of a vacuum, but, rather, circulate within our dance communities and build upon the stories of others. Our experiences as just two dancers are but a drop in the bucket, but we have been validated in talking with each other and with peers to learn that we are not isolated, but part of a community of dance practitioners who have felt excluded from mainstream dance spaces for various reasons.

This book is the result of many hours of consistent conversation and collaborative writing between the two of us over more than four years. Throughout this process, we have discovered how each other's worldviews have been shaped, as well as our individual trigger points. We started with discussions about dance and racism, which led us to question the polarization of ideals, belief systems, and frameworks of understanding that supposedly define who we are within the constellation of dance as a field. Our conversations revealed the vulnerabilities and insecurities that arise from our cultural and racialized experiences. For example, Sinclair has felt uneasy about sharing anecdotes from memory that seem "non-intellectual," having been told that his embodied experience as a Black African man is not rigorous research. Kate has been apprehensive about sharing elements of her research on dance cultures other than the ones associated with her skin color, ethnicity, or nationality, for fear of being accused of cultural appropriation as a White American woman. The process of digging into our memories and emotions has been a different kind of challenge than traditional research, in which we would be expected to distance or remove ourselves from the work. We have come to view the dance knowledge that both of us have gathered throughout our lives as a valid form of research, and this book is meant to offer a model for collaborative dance research in which bodies, memories, emotions, and even doubts are fully present.

We also want to resist preconceptions about what academic dance writing should be, precisely because dance is felt in the body. Dance is personal, physical, and emotional. We often are pressured to write about dance within a specific academic framework, but we feel strongly that over-intellectualizing our experiences as a way to make people feel more comfortable downplays how the anecdotes we share in the following chapters are, at times, difficult and raw. As Sally Ann Ness demonstrates in "Dancing in the Field: Notes from Memory" (1993), writing about dance is a process that starts with the experience, which is based in the individual body and is refined through a process of drafts that become increasingly distanced from that initial experience. We want to stay as close to our unedited initial experiences as we can, fully aware that doing so reveals much about our own biases and vulnerabilities.

To do so, we resist an over-reliance on the formalized and visual aspects of dance and instead foreground the individual, embodied experience with its perceptual organization of various visual, auditory, and kinesthetic elements. In so doing, we look to the work of anthropologist and dance pioneer Katherine Dunham and cultural anthropologist Ruth Landes, two women who centered the body and individual experience in their scholarly work, resisting pressures to maintain so-called "scientific objectivity" that ruled the field of anthropology in the middle of the twentieth century, as is evident in their writings about their embodied experiences as women researchers in the Caribbean and Brazil (Dunham 1946, 1969; Landes 1986, 1994). We also draw on performance studies scholar Diana Taylor's theory of the archive and the repertoire (2003) to consider what performance and the body can teach us about people and their cultural histories. We recognize the power and agency of so many meaning-makers and movers across the world, working in a vast array of forms, traditions, and communities, who are not always recognized for their contributions to dance.

Finally, an important goal throughout this book is to reveal both of our positionalities through our storytelling to describe how we, Sinclair and Kate, navigate the world as dancers and educators. While we are writing this book together because we share many perspectives on the field of dance today, we come at these issues from very different experiences that are shaped by our race, ethnicity, nationality, gender, and more. We are aware that some things written in this book would sound reasonable coming from one of us, but problematic coming from another. We must point out that the stakes are higher for Sinclair, who faces instability and discrimination every day due to his racial identity and immigration status in the United States. One of the difficulties of writing about dance is how disembodied it is. Often, the assumptions that we make about a person and what they are saying or doing are shaped by their voice or body. The body is neither seen nor heard in writing and so we are cautious about what assumptions you, the reader, will have while reading these words coming from one or both of us. In these moments, we aim to be clear about who is speaking versus when we are speaking together with one unified voice. Throughout each chapter, we weave in and out of individual interludes told in the first-person; dialogues staged between us; and joint writing to demonstrate the ways that our voices shift when we are remembering a personal experience; talking about an experience in conversation with one another; or narrating to our readers. The dialogue sections were the hardest to write, partly because we were tempted to edit out the uncertainties and vulnerabilities that arose in our conversations. We kept many of those raw, emotional moments so as not to mask our process of learning and collaboration.

We write to spark a conversation about equity and inclusion in dance among students and educators alike who work in any form, as well as researchers who study dance communities around the world. This book primarily presents examples from various African and African diasporic dance forms, Brazilian and East Caribbean dance, and Irish and other percussive dance forms, due to our areas of expertise. We recognize that many dances are not represented here, and we hope that this book will serve as an impetus for more dancers from other parts of the world to add their voices to this conversation. We also have chosen to focus on the interactions between race, ethnicity, nationality, and culture, setting aside the complexities that gender, sexuality, class, and other social identities bring to the conversation until we can expand on our framework in future research.

We believe our work is a valuable resource for dance educators and institutions of arts and culture, as well as performance venues seeking ways to diversify their curation processes. With our particular focus on the body and how dancers approach the challenges of describing and experiencing embodied culture, we also see our framework for cultural confluences as applicable to more fields than just dance, such as music, performance studies, anthropology, and archaeology. Ultimately, this book takes an optimistic, yet realistic and practical, stance on how dance can be part of the solution to creating more equitable and inclusive spaces. Rather than focus on what is excluded from mainstream dance spaces, we highlight how the inclusion of a wider variety of dance cultures and their associated aesthetic systems and philosophies add value to our understanding of what dance can be.

In this book

Throughout this book, we discuss the challenges of communicating the value of various dances in our framework of cultural confluences within five spheres of analysis: (1) language and brand markings in dance; (2) aesthetic value systems; (3) space and cultural transposition in dance; (4) steps, choreography, and improvisation in the creative process; and (5) archiving and research in dance academia. Chapter 1 deals with the limitations of current language to talk about non-mainstream dance forms in academic settings, as well as possibilities for expanding this language by establishing the need to identify value and branding; understanding the creation of memes and heuristics; exploring issues of cultural appropriation in the transmission of dance forms; and examining dance as play. We consider definitions of dance terms in the realm of ballet and modern forms in mainstream spaces, and we discuss some of the challenges of "translating" dance in new settings.

Chapter 2 focuses on aesthetics and how technique is defined and evaluated in different dance cultures. We consider what dance can achieve and enact in relation to the agency that practitioners have, and we consider the role of the body itself in transmitting aesthetic value and communal knowledge through movement. How do we define the "essence" of a dance technique, and how do we determine what is "good" or "bad" aesthetically? Do all dance cultures necessarily involve "judging" the aesthetic value of dance, or are there also situations in which dance just "is?" Chapter 3 builds on this discussion of aesthetics to describe how spatial configurations in mainstream academic or concert dance settings are fundamentally at odds with the community-based settings of many culturally specific dance forms. When Sinclair walks into a dance studio to teach African dance, sees a piano in the corner, and is told not to drum too loudly, for example, he immediately understands that this space is meant for someone else. How can we include other dances and dancers in spaces that were designed for ballet and modern dance? Is it possible to transpose alternative understandings of space outside of the communal settings from which so many non-mainstream dance forms arise? What opportunities do we have as artists to not only redesign these spaces but also curate them in ways that invite our communities in? We focus on the use of space in the classroom and performance, and we demonstrate how spaces might be reconfigured in more inclusive ways through pedagogical and creative design choices.

Chapter 4 explores the concepts of choreography and improvisation, which are sometimes presented as being at odds with one another, but which are, we argue, constantly in dialogue. We explain the ways that "just steps" are diminished in studies of traditional dance forms for which steps are transmitted and repeated as patterns of meaning from teacher to student or peer to peer across generations. We compare "just steps" in traditional forms to "task-based" choreography in postmodern concert dance (Chaleff 2018). We discuss how being told that our traditional steps are simple, repetitive, and monotonous ultimately reduces the value of our dance forms, associating them with the "archaic" or the "primitive," suggesting they lack refinement or innovation. We offer some ideas about how to expand perspectives on how dance creates cultural meaning, acknowledging that the value of kinesthetic knowledge systems may be difficult or impossible to verbalize.

Finally, Chapter 5 is about adapting more inclusive frameworks for research on dance cultures that better reflect embodied processes of archiving and cultural knowledge production in dance. We reflect on the role of dance as a receptacle for archival memory and community building across space and time. We look at dance as an archive and how the body contains the knowledge of a community that cannot—and often should not—be written down. Our institutions are so focused on words, ideas that can be verbalized or written, and conventional or literary notions of storytelling, that the body itself is ignored. Dancers, in general, tend to acknowledge such body knowledge, but we find that our field has developed few methods of analysis beyond a limited range of embodied epistemologies. In attempting to talk about or write about dance, there is always an imperfect translation, and so we also explore how technology might be able to support the visualization and analysis of dance migrations on individual and cultural levels.

Throughout this book, we discuss the need for systemic change in how dance scholarship and artistic practice are configured in our institutional structures. Simple inclusion is not enough. Through our framework of cultural confluences, we call for a reconsideration of how "intellect" and cultural knowledge show up in many different types of bodies as they migrate throughout various spaces. Certainly, dancers, of all people, understand the concept of a "mind" that pervades the body as a whole—and how embodied knowledge concerns not just the individual body, but also the body of an entire community, composed of people who share values and beliefs but also come with their own perspectives and idiosyncrasies of movement. We make a point of highlighting diversity within particular dance cultures, not just between them. The embodied narratives that arise from such danced expressions provide an alternate form of history that centers on those common values and every so often, also exposes the conflicts, tensions, and disagreements that exist in those histories. Both continuities and ruptures are crucial for understanding a community and its culture. This book encourages us to move through the nuances and contradictions that inevitably arise in living, breathing embodied practices.

References

Adichie, Chimamanda Ngozi. 2009. *The Danger of a Single Story*. TEDGlobal. https://www.ted.com/talks/chimamanda_ngozi_adichie_the_danger_of_a_single_story.

Bhabha, Homi K. 2011. "Culture's In-Between." In *Questions of Cultural Identity*, edited by Stuart Hall and Paul du Gay, 53–60. London, UK: SAGE Publications. https://doi.org/10.4135/9781446221907.

Catanese, Brandi Wilkins. 2011. *The Problem of the Color(Blind): Racial Transgression and the Politics of Black Performance*. Theater—Theory/Text/Performance. Ann Arbor, MI: University of Michigan Press.

Chakravorty, Pallabi. 2000. "From Interculturalism to Historicism: Reflections on Classical Indian Dance." *Dance Research Journal* 32 (2): 108–19.

Chaleff, Rebecca. 2018. "Activating Whiteness: Racializing the Ordinary in US American Postmodern Dance." *Dance Research Journal* 50 (3): 71–84. https://doi.org/10.1017/S0149767718000372.

Chang, Heewon. 2008. *Autoethnography as Method*. Developing Qualitative Inquiry. Walnut Creek, CA: Left Coast Press.

Conquergood, Dwight Lorne. 2013. *Cultural Struggles: Performance, Ethnography, Praxis*, edited by E. Patrick Johnson. Ann Arbor, MI: University of Michigan Press.

Crenshaw, Kimberlé. 1989. "Demarginalizing the Intersection of Race and Sex: A Black Feminist Critique of Antidiscrimination Doctrine, Feminist Theory and Antiracist Politics." *University of Chicago Legal Forum* 1989 (1): 139–67.

Davis, Crystal U. 2022. *Dance and Belonging: Implicit Bias and Inclusion in Dance Education*. Jefferson, NC: McFarland.

Dunham, Katherine. 1946. *Journey to Accompong*. New York, NY: Henry Holt and Company.
———. 1969. *Island Possessed*. Chicago, IL: University of Chicago Press.
Hall, Stuart. 2011. "Introduction: Who Needs 'Identity'?" In *Questions of Cultural Identity*, edited by Stuart Hall and Paul du Gay, 1–17. London, UK: SAGE Publications. https://doi.org/10.4135/9781446221907.
Kealiinohomoku, Joann Wheeler. 1972. "Folk Dance." In *Folklore & Folklife: An Introduction*, edited by Richard M. Dorson. Chicago, IL: University of Chicago Press.
Landes, Ruth. 1986. "A Woman Anthropologist in Brazil." In *Women in the Field: Anthropological Experiences*, edited by Peggy Golde, 119–39. Berkeley, CA: University of California Press.
———. 1994. *The City of Women*. Albuquerque, NM: University of New Mexico Press.
Madison, D. Soyini. 2020. *Critical Ethnography: Method, Ethics, and Performance*. Third edition. Thousand Oaks, CA: SAGE Publications.
Ness, Sally Ann. 1993. "Dancing in the Field: Notes from Memory." In *Corporealities: Dancing Knowledge, Culture and Power*, edited by Susan Leigh Foster, 129–54. London, UK: Routledge.
Ojaide, Tanure. 2001. "Poetry, Performance, and Art: Udje Dance Songs of Nigeria's Urhobo People." *Research in African Literatures* 32 (2): 44–75. https://doi.org/10.1353/ral.2001.0058.
Pratt, Mary Louise. 1991. "Arts of the Contact Zone." *Profession*, 33–40.
Savigliano, Marta. 2009. "Worlding Dance and Dancing Out There in the World." In *Worlding Dance*, edited by Susan Leigh Foster, 163–90. Basingstoke, NY: Palgrave Macmillan.
Taylor, Diana. 2003. *The Archive and the Repertoire: Performing Cultural Memory in the Americas*. Durham, NC: Duke University Press.
White, Luise. 2000. *Speaking with Vampires: Rumor and History in Colonial Africa*. Studies on the History of Society and Culture. Berkeley, CA: University of California Press.
Wolf, Eric R. 1982. *Europe and the People without History*. Berkeley, CA: University of California Press.

1 Language, value, and branding in confluent dance spaces

In this chapter, we focus on language that is commonly used in academia today to describe dance and how that language does not fully capture non-mainstream dance forms, who practices them, and what value they bring to the field. In the United States, this language often arises from mainstream cultural aesthetics—specifically from ballet and modern dance—and does not always reflect the value of other aesthetic systems. Attitudes, biases, and assumptions about the value of a dance form arise from the use of reductive words, terminologies, categories such as "world dance" or "global dance," and binaries like Western and non-Western, Black and White, and African and European. The attitudes that develop because of this language result in exclusionary practices and inequitable treatment throughout our field, from the classroom to performance spaces. This language deters practitioners from forms outside of the perceived "mainstream" (as defined in the Introduction), keeping them from growing and progressing, and even heightening conflicts, competition, and divisions among dancers, creating a sort of scarcity model in dance communities where resources are already few and far between. Our language needs to be revised so that it speaks to the value that many different types of dancers and movers bring to our field and promotes the inclusion of more dance forms and aesthetic systems.

Our cultural confluences framework describes how encounters within shared spaces produce, shape, and absorb ever-shifting mainstream and non-mainstream currents. Within confluent dance spaces, we see the interaction of a few dominant mainstream cultures alongside many non-mainstream cultures, all of which compete for the same pool of resources. The idea of confluent spaces in dance builds on Mary Louise Pratt's notion of "contact zones," which she describes as "social spaces where cultures meet, clash, and grapple with each other, often in contexts of highly asymmetrical relations of power" (1991, 34). Our notion of a confluent space is partly about negotiating power struggles, privilege, and other sociopolitical dynamics. However, it also accounts for the more migratory experience of feeling a certain amount of privilege in one environment or moment in time and then moving or shifting one's perspective and feeling less privileged or more marginalized. The idea of moving through these confluences and being able to experience both the mainstream and non-mainstream at once is an apt description

DOI: 10.4324/9781003231226-2

of dance as a physical and philosophical vehicle through which a person or community comes to understand itself. Unlike the contact zone, which information scientist Robin Boast points out is ultimately a "site in and for the center" (2011, 67), confluences have no center and resist rules that produce the generalization and standardization of a form. Being in the mainstream feels liberating and powerful, able to push through with strong currents of influence, whereas being in the non-mainstream feels like being pushed out or trapped by the dominant streams that hold one in place.

A single dancer can be both mainstream and non-mainstream at the same time, depending on one's environment and perspective. For example, Sinclair recalls having a certain amount of privilege and authority as a dancer at home in Nigeria, but he concurrently finds himself at a disadvantage and discriminated against as a Black dancer in the United States. He brings a sense of authority and confidence with him from Nigeria but must continually navigate his new positionality as a marginalized dancer in the United States. Although as an Urhobo person he is a cultural minority in Nigeria, his university degree places him in the mainstream Nigerian elite dance scene. He graduated from the University of Benin and went on to work with the State Arts Council, a premier cultural troupe in Benin, Edo State. He worked not just as a dancer, but also as a choreographer who was commissioned to direct and choreograph for the 2012 Nigerian National Arts Festival (NAFEST). This revered position gave him a voice within the dance community in Edo, offering him privilege as part of the mainstream at both organizational and cultural levels at home. Being an immigrant dancer in the United States is a stark contrast for him.

In a different example, Kate has also been aware of the push and pull inherent to being mainstream and non-mainstream at the same time. When she thinks back to her teenage years as an Irish dancer, she remembers how she could not compete for the same scholarships as her high school classmates who practiced ballet, simply because Irish dance was not recognized as "real" or "serious" dance. However, her friend who grew up doing Scottish Highland dancing at a nearby high school remembers being jealous of how much more attention and respect Irish dancers got—how much "cooler" they seemed. There were much higher numbers of participants in Irish dance and more institutional resources to support organizations, competitions, and performances. In comparison to ballet, Irish dance is non-mainstream, but, since Riverdance popularized Irish dance in the mid-1990s, it is more widely practiced and more mainstream than Scottish Highland dancing in the United States. Thus, one can feel diminished while looking in one direction but feel privileged when turning around to look in another. We carry multiple such realities within us simultaneously.

This journey between mainstream and non-mainstream experiences relates to how we navigate various spaces as dancers. Migration, diaspora, and the experience of displacement from a particular place to a new one can be both a disquieting and liberating venture. In dance, displacement is reflected in a dancer's difficulties with practicing in new spaces and environments and in the different expectations held by audiences, gatekeepers, and fellow artists about a dance form. Savigliano describes how "relocalized translation" is required for dancers from specific cultures who enter into academia and "must *talk* willing dance students and curious scholars *into* valuing and recognizing the form that they embody and practice" (2009, 180, emphasis in original). Language—along with cultural attitudes, customs, and etiquette—sets the stage for how migratory dancers navigate the experience of relocation. Geographical and cultural distance also produces gaps in communication and creates a disconnect from local sociopolitical issues. Moving to a new environment and becoming non-mainstream after experiencing the mainstream also comes with losing a sense of community—as in the case of Sinclair moving from Nigeria to the United States, becoming a racial minority, and dealing with heightened stereotypes about being Black and African. Constant migration between the mainstream and non-mainstream can feel like being caught in "nowhere," without a clear sense of direction or purpose, and feeling uncertain about how much power one really holds.

We see a connection between the ways that our identities as dancers from specific dance cultures have been shaped by our own migrations. We have both experienced the uprooting and transposition of cultural practices from the "homeland" into a new space in which many other cultures compete for attention and resources. Whereas some cultural practices "at home" seem normal and quotidian, they become hyper-valued in the diaspora. A dance may also become idealized and exoticized to an extent in the context of migration. The diasporic space in particular demands translation, and maintaining tradition and authenticity becomes a heightened concern for dancers who must also navigate assimilation, segregation, and alienation. Dances are frequently extracted from their cultural contexts to create workout classes or to present virtuosic performances on stage, setting aside other cultural aspects like food, songs, and language, all of which also constitute the foundation of these dance communities' identities. In addition, the extent to which a dance culture has assimilated into the mainstream or adopts characteristics from the dominant aesthetic largely determines to what extent that dance form is accepted by mainstream audiences and, as a result, how practitioners receive resources, opportunities, and recognition.

Sinclair feels like he is living at the intersection of "nowhere" between two dichotomies—the United States and Nigeria, as well as Western and non-Western dance. He is uneasy about the term "diaspora" because, to him, it denotes a state of alienation. For many tangible and emotional reasons, being a recent immigrant in the United States forces him to be in a position where he has to sometimes uphold and defend his culture of origin. He has also had to accept his geographical shift and displacement. He feels caught between two conflicting worlds that will not accept his knowledge about dance. He is often expected to negotiate how Black he can be and how much of his colonial self he can display. For example, in his work, "Kaleidoscope of Tuts," presented at the John F. Kennedy Center for the Performing Arts in 2020, he examined the lived experiences of Black men in Nigeria compared to Black men in the United States. In staging this work performed by mostly American dancers, he struggled to contextualize the process and present specific Nigerian political ideologies to American audiences. In addition, as a person from the Urhobo community, a specific cultural group in Nigeria, his dancing is not even mainstream in his home country. (There are about 10 million Urhobo people out of more than 200 million people in Nigeria, who are majority Yoruba, Igbo, and Hausa.) Generally speaking, Urhobos are lumped into a collective minority group that makes smaller groups less visible on a national level. This is why Sinclair feels "mainstream" from an intellectual/educational standpoint, but non-mainstream in terms of cultural representation on national and international levels. His feeling of being non-mainstream in the United States stems from the fact that not only is Nigerian culture unfamiliar here, but also his Urhobo community is even lesser known than more prominent cultural groups like the Yoruba, Igbo, and Hausa.

Kate, on the other hand, experiences migration in a different way, having been born and raised in the United States with strong cultural connections to her Irish and Greek heritages. Unlike Sinclair's feelings of diasporic alienation, she was encouraged to embrace her diasporic experience growing up, which made her feel more connected to her ancestry, especially in light of the United States' celebration of multiculturalism in the 1980s and 1990s. She was always aware of the connections between her dancing and her Irish identity, especially because relatively few non-Irish people were dancing in the early 1990s, before Riverdance made Irish dancing a global practice. She remembers being amazed when she went to the World Championships in Ireland for the first time in 1994 and arrived at the hotel to see a space in which Irish dancing was completely normal, understood, and celebrated. At the same time, however, she was well aware, even at a young age, that her Americanness set her apart and that her team was at a disadvantage at this event due to her school's lack of access to Irish trainers and choreographers. When she went back to Ireland for graduate school in Irish dance, she felt in her element in a place where Irish dance served as the basis for training in the academy. However, she also felt her Americanness come through again when one of her teachers told her that she would never fully understand Irish dance rhythm because she did not grow up in Ireland. This prompted a bit of a crisis about her identity as an Irish dancer and a sense of isolation with no foundation to stand on.

These examples of how cultural confluences can produce feelings of instability and uncertainty help us describe the ways that everyone migrates through different spaces while engaging with different cultural forms throughout their lives. We can think of migration in a geographical sense, but we can also think about it in terms of the ways that we develop our identities as dancers through the people and cultures we encounter along the way. The challenge is to find language that allows us as dancers to address the nuances of confluence and migration, while also being specific and direct in descriptions of our work. The following sections delve into how brand markers represent value in dance and simultaneously uphold barriers and limitations for dancers from non-mainstream forms. We examine the language that is used in scholarship and teaching to promote such labels and heighten fears about cultural appropriation. We believe that sometimes this language does more harm to the development of our forms than it does to protect them.

Value and branding in dance

The separation between mainstream and non-mainstream in our framework of cultural confluences is defined by value and capital, which are both, in turn, defined by the labels and brands used to describe dance. Branding comes into play when selling components of specific cultural practices, as in processes of national, racial, ethnic, or cultural identity formation. On the positive side, the capitalist system has afforded dancers in the United States the structure to self-sustain their dance practices, in contrast with a government-sponsored system like that of Nigeria, which struggles to keep dancers working and making a living. We recognize the benefits that capitalism may bring to dance artists, but we are concerned that what we as dancers produce as cultural experiences have come to be solely defined as products to be consumed under a capitalist system. The simplification and categorization of dance forms and their culturally based aesthetic value systems essentially "brands" a dance form with words intended to sell a product or an idea. According to Keller and Lehmann, "At their most basic level, brands serve as markers for the offerings of a firm. For customers, brands can simplify choice, promise a particular quality level, reduce risk, and/or engender trust" (2006, 740). In the context of dance, branding is the use of a particular name or phrase to describe a creative work or experience in dance, often denoted by genre or style. Components used to brand a dance form might include specific dance steps, costuming, or instruments that are "traditional" and used to sell an image and promote social cohesion or unite a community around a shared goal. Artists rely on such language to conceptualize and contextualize their practices, make money, and build their reputations. For example, West African dancers may be recognizable by colorful *lapa* cloths and djembe accompaniment, or Irish dancers by their intricately embroidered *Book of Kells* inspired costumes and accordion accompaniment. Such elements offer quality control, sponsorship of community artists, and the documentation of special cultural practices for posterity, which in turn legitimizes the form as it becomes visible and recognizable.

Brand names are used to determine how dancers and dances are valued. In *Valuing Dance*, Susan Leigh Foster sets up a framework of commodity and gift to describe how dance value is "exchanged" (2019). While this framework works well for dance forms that have become mainstream or commodified in certain ways—which Foster demonstrates through examples of ballet, modern, jazz, and Native American powwow in a cultural tourism setting—it establishes dance as something that is always transactional. The examples that Foster highlights in her book largely demonstrate the value of dance in the global marketplace. Savigliano also emphasizes that understanding the market—formed by consumption, commodity, globalization, cosmopolitanism, and capitalism—is central to understanding the concept of "world dance" (2009). The marketplace is a primary factor in creating the categories and brands that our field uses today to assign value in dance, and we are beholden to the rules created for us by this system. Looking at the arts marketplace, dance is usually packaged using easily identifiable, sometimes stereotypical, labels so that audiences can buy into it and be entertained by it.

That is, an arts manager or dance curator uses language that will sell tickets. For example, we saw an ad for a hybrid ballet and hip-hop performance that touted the "sophistication" of classical dance alongside the "raw energy" of street dance. This may sound like an exotic and exciting performance that people would want to buy tickets for, but these words prompt all kinds of assumptions and biases about what these two dance forms are and how we value them. What is the trade-off for this kind of language that brands dancers using reductive categories and descriptors?

Foster also mentions dialogues and transfers of energy that occur through what she terms "gift exchange" in dance. In many Nigerian cultures, for example, dance is not only a creative practice but it can also be used for exchange, along with food and precious items like kola nuts, silvers, and high-value alcoholic drinks, or to perform legislative and executive duties within society. However, we can also move past the transactional to consider how a dance experience (not necessarily a "performance") can make a participant feel fulfilled, safe, protected, or appreciative. There is a sort of exchange here, to be sure, but it does not require the marketplace's input and is not defined by what is received in return. We find this aspect to be crucial for those living in a state of migration or dislocation in order to find a sense of community through dance. This book is filled with examples of our personal experiences in which the market was not necessarily present (or at least not top of mind). We use these examples to develop language to build on Foster's framework and think further about how we speak about and apportion value in dance. Is it possible to consider the value of confluent dance cultures outside of the language of marketplace and exchange? Does the market underlie every interaction we have in dance? Can we expand beyond brands, hierarchies, and binary categories? We are interested in developing language beyond simplistic brand markers to account for the limitless nuance required to more fully examine the value that different forms bring to the dance field.

Memes and heuristics

Dancers and dance scholars have often used language as an analogy to talk about dance structures and vocabularies (e.g., Kaeppler 1972; Royce 1977; Williams 1979, 1999; Copeland and Cohen 1983; Foster 1986; Foley 2012; Preston-Dunlop 1995; Bannerman 2014). Both of us are drawn to this analogy, but, as many of these scholars have also expressed, we are cautious of it because we believe so much is expressed nonverbally or pre-linguistically through movement, especially in forms of dance that center around community practice. The term "body language," in particular, diminishes complex transfers of embodied knowledge that are often culturally defined processes. These processes both replicate ideas and generate new ones. If we think about "steps" as a sort of movement "vocabulary" or "phrase," as often described in academic dance circles, we are tempted to think of dance as expressing only certain types of intellectual ideas. Using this terminology may limit the possibility of thinking about how movements allow us to express in ways that cannot be verbalized or intellectualized (as discussed by

Hanna 1987; Sklar 1991). We are interested in how value in dance arises from non-verbal embodied expressions across a variety of dance cultures.

Imitation or mimesis is central to dance transmission, which we can define as the transfer of aesthetic values from one body to another. In *The Meme Machine*, Susan Blackmore describes imitation as an important human skill. Using the term "meme," coined by Richard Dawkins in 1976 to describe a form of genetic replicator, she explains, "When you imitate someone else, something is passed on. This 'something' can then be passed on again, and again, and so take on a life of its own." She maintains that we might call this meme "an idea, an instruction, a behaviour, a piece of information" (1999, 4).[1] In the context of dance, a "meme" arises from the process of using sensory data to imitate, embody, transpose, and transmit information such that the dance gains a life of its own.

Memes in dance are movement patterns and steps, which, when imitated, actively transfer body knowledge, the value of the dance, and its associated cultural worldviews. Throughout the world, individuals learn to dance using memes that are repeatable actions and customs delivered in the form of transferable cues, signals, attitudes, and behaviors that help them learn, engage, and perform. Memes are so often repeated that they become second nature within the specific context of the dance and in the broader cultural context within which it is practiced. In many cultures, these strategies often lack documentation, codification, or other forms of written or spoken language to reinforce them. The role of memes in dance transmission is important when considering the value of dance steps and patterns and the ways the dancers build embodied archives and memories, as we describe in more detail in Chapters 4 and 5.

Learning to dance in a new space, however, is never just a simple imitation, and the process becomes complicated in migratory contexts. As dance ethnographer Yolanda Van Ede explains in the context of the transcultural relocation of Spanish flamenco in Japan: "... the embedding of [a] genre into a new sociocultural environment requires adjustments to both the pre-existing ways of learning in the new environment as well as to the new meaning the genre may have ..." (2014, 61). She describes how the "sensory ranking" in Japan is different from that of Spain, meaning that in Japanese dance, students imitate first by sight, whereas dancers in Spain focus primarily on the sonic and tactile. This is an example of how the transcultural practice of a dance form in a confluent space outside of its origin is shaped by economic and social transitions that complicate the ways we think about imitation and migration in different cultures. Imitation results in certain changes in the body of the person doing the imitating, but those changes are also shaped by how that person perceives and then expresses that information through their body. All of this is also shaped by their cultural aesthetics and worldview. Thus, our framework of cultural confluences necessitates a discussion about how dance affects us and how we behave as a result of that influence as we move through various spaces, which we describe in more detail in the following chapter about adopting and expressing aesthetic value through dance.

To maintain some form of continuity in confluent spaces, practitioners rely on cultural codes in order to read and interpret what they experience. The legibility of certain cultural "codes" in dance tends to lend legitimacy to a form. For example, in academia, we have noticed that ballet, with its highly structured transmission systems and accompanying language, is treated as more valuable than dances that do not rely on a formalized vocabulary. Dance forms that have not been codified to a great extent may be deemed illegible if outsiders or newcomers cannot decipher what is going on in a performance or at a dance event without the verbal or visual clues that help to structure meaning in the Western dance framework. For example, in 2021, the two of us presented a cross-cultural exploration of Brazilian, Nigerian, and Irish music and dance at a performance venue outside of Washington, D.C. One person who was an outsider to all three of these cultures described our work as "just an improvisational dance jam" and questioned the rigor of our creative process, despite the years of cultural knowledge and intentional creative decisions that we brought to the space (we expand on this case study in Chapter 3). This person did not understand the context and did not pick up on the cultural cues we presented. It is one thing to see dancing and not understand what is going on because one does not "speak" the language, but it is another thing to say that a dance is not valuable just because one cannot understand it. The idea of illegibility goes hand-in-hand with erasure in the sense that non-mainstream dance that cannot be translated into mainstream language risks erasure or delegitimization in that space.

We do not believe, however, that more codification of dance languages is a solution to this problem. We have seen how the codification of a previously informal and uncodified dance practice can threaten its continuity. When codification leads to more legitimacy, there are always some who are left behind. Those who continue to practice outside of this codified system may not be considered "legitimate" or "authentic," and may become marginalized for not adopting the accepted system. In Chapter 4, we delve into the issue of codification *vis-à-vis* improvisation (which we do not see as mutually exclusive practices) and the perception that improvised dance is less serious because it does not seem structured or codified. The perceived illegibility of non-mainstream dances that have not been codified in ways that comply with mainstream standards makes it difficult to have meaningful conversations about them, and so we need to use new language that addresses such value in academic and professional dance spaces.

The legibility of a dance in a Western context is often defined by how well it can be described in mainstream language, or how well it can be described in any language at all. In fact, the idea of talking about dance, as opposed to just dancing, can seem foreign to some. Sinclair remembers early on in his graduate school career, in the months after arriving from Nigeria, that one of his professors took him to see several modern dance performances. After each one, his professor asked, "What did you think about the dance?" The question puzzled him, and he would always simply reply, "It was a really good performance." After a few of these outings, his professor joked that it seemed like he liked every dance he saw. It was then that Sinclair realized that he had never before considered the idea of "liking" a dance performance. He did not have the language to elaborate because it had never occurred to him whether he should like it or not. In his culture, dance is not evaluated in this way. The idea of a "good" or "bad" dance performance was foreign to him and he did not know how to distinguish the two. He realized that the Western academic system that he found himself in was entirely based on critique and metrics of "good" and "bad." To understand this distinction means that one is technically sound and well-trained. Although academic language in any field must be learned, we have found that the language used to talk about non-mainstream dance cultures in academia not only misdescribes them but often omits the very elements that bring value to those forms. Within the spectrum of "good" dance training are myriad formulated codes that students, audiences, and teachers are trained to know for them to be classified as educated dancers within the mainstream system. In the following chapters, we elaborate on the ways that, in some cultures, a space and its associated social customs are constructed in such a way that value is not determined in a binary system of "good" and "bad," but according to other less tangible and delineated criteria.

In the past, certain heuristics have placed value on Westernized dance aesthetics such as verticality, uprightness, extension, pointed feet, etc., as "good," whereas dances that do not follow those aesthetic values would be "bad" or "wrong."[2] More recently, these same heuristics are being used in the U.S. arts and culture sector to expand much-needed equity and diversity efforts such that techniques that contrast with so-called Western aesthetics with attributes like groundedness, release, curves, etc., are also valued and recognized. While we support this effort, we are also concerned with the ways that simplistic rules have emerged that help people make quick judgments based on the same binary language and aesthetic categories that have always been in effect without considering the complexity of what equity and diversity mean from culture to culture. In preserving this system, those making decisions may not understand a dance culture's values beyond visual aesthetics or political identities, or how they are different from binary approaches to evaluating dance scholarship and practice. These heuristics require people to fit neatly into boxes and categories based on racial and ethnic markers that make it easier for us to understand and judge (and hire or fund). In the real world, however, we find immense complexity and even contradiction in the ways that dance cultures "abide" by these heuristic rules, as we describe in more detail in Chapter 5. Such "mental shortcuts" help decision makers push diversity and inclusion efforts forward, but at what cost? Who or what is left unconsidered when using simplistic heuristics to decide what is valuable? Judgment systems and a lack of understanding of non-mainstream cultural value systems set the stage for negative feedback loops and unproductive conversations around progress in the dance field today.

Racialized branding in dance

The language used to describe dance can be constraining or expansive. Our field relies on aesthetic categories to help us organize and judge the world around us and reduce complex ideas and cultural phenomena into simpler, and often simplistic, terms. We believe that the limiting categories that have been created to organize the dance field have formed an impossible framework for dancers from non-mainstream cultures to navigate. Restrictive terminology boxes dance artists like us into sociopolitical identities that arise from one's race, ethnicity, gender, and class. As a result, this language forms barriers as to how people can engage with dances of their own and others' cultures. We agree that dance is political—the body is political—and that politics are necessary in the fight for equity, but we also believe that the politicized language that boxes us into categories does not adequately reflect our lived experiences as bodies moving through shared spaces. Essentialist thinking pressures us to stay in our "lanes" and prove our worth to outsiders while also carrying our traditions and protecting our practices from cultural appropriation. Such thinking leaves little freedom to navigate confluent streams and collaborate in ways that could potentially benefit our work. We are looking for more expansive and generative language that can help us create more inclusive aesthetic systems and spatial configurations in academia.

While language can be used to uplift and communicate value, it can also be used to activate bias. People use words to relay what they do or do not value, and then they pass these values on to other people through teaching, dancing, and other social interactions. So much of the language used today to talk about dance and dancers is based on appearance—skin color, physical features, what we wear, how we carry ourselves, etc.—and relates to how one's physical appearance is defined politically. This is natural because dance is a physical, embodied form. Dance *is* the body. All kinds of assumptions arise about a person while looking at their moving body. We know that some people look at each one of us as dancers and immediately assume that Sinclair does "African dance" or "Black dance" and that Kate is "just" a "dancer," unqualified by race, ethnicity, or culture. That is, Sinclair is branded as "Black" and "African" and Kate as "White" (often, an unmarked category), and thus we become subject to the assumptions that are associated with these stereotypes. Sinclair must explain that he does more than what the insufficient definitions of African dance or Black dance suggest he does. And Kate must explain how she comes from a very specific dance culture—a specific kind of "White" dance.

These experiences prompt us to push back on the aforementioned binary frameworks created to describe "Africanist"/"Black" or "Europeanist"/"White" dance forms that we see in current diversity initiatives in our field because neither of us feels that we fit squarely into these categories. "African dance" does not capture the fullness and diversity of dance cultures on the African continent, just as "White dance" and "European dance" are vague and nonspecific categories that are more diverse than their racial or geographic labels. In addition, an "African dancer," as one is commonly imagined, is not necessarily the same as a "dancer from Africa," just as not all dancers who are White practice ballet or modern dance. We feel this should be obvious, but we are continually surprised by how ubiquitous these assumptions are and how much energy it takes to fight against them.

We are both affected by the oppositional language that describes White or European and Black or African aesthetics. The stereotype of the White, Europeanist aesthetic is often described with words such as vertical, outward, upward, control, and order, with toes pointed, feet turned out, and legs extended, whereas the Black, Africanist aesthetic is often described as grounded, inward, free, improvised, and released, with feet flat on the ground and knees bent. These descriptions may seem relatively neutral and may even be accurate in general, but they are subject to many exceptions that cannot be ignored or brushed aside. Other words used to stereotype and create aesthetic hierarchies among dance forms include clean vs. rough, refined vs. raw, and tame or disciplined vs. frenzied, wild, feverish, animalistic, loud, or noisy. These binaries and hierarchies are often racially based, but can also be based on class or socioeconomics, as in the case of so-called "folk" forms *vis-à-vis* classical forms in various cultures. Such branding controls dancers and trivializes what they do, how their traditions evolved, and how they are contextualized, neatly packaging them for consumption. We also see a separation of dance as play ("a good workout" or a "fun improvisational jam") from "serious" artistic practice, in which the former is diminished as simply recreational, as we describe later in this chapter and in more depth in Chapter 4. Such categorization and hierarchization have been used to form and justify divisions between cultural groups and their aesthetic systems, creating value terms for some forms while devaluing others.

There is a history of differentiating between White, Europeanist and Black, Africanist dance forms as two extremes of a binary aesthetic system. Brenda Dixon-Gottschild's books, *Digging the Africanist Presence in American Performance* (1998) and *The Black Dancing Body* (2003), are important contributions to dance studies that recuperate the African diasporic influences that have been ignored and unacknowledged in American modern dance. Her argument is built upon a theoretical binary of Europeanist and Africanist aesthetic extremes, in which the former is described as vertical, upright, sterile, and controlled, and the latter as grounded, curved, sensual, and released. She acknowledges that she draws on generic, stereotypical descriptions for the purposes of her argument, and yet she stops before delving into the nuances of dancing between these extremes. We believe that associating such highly charged words with racialized aesthetics within one or a few forms reinforces these stereotypes and contributes to the formation of a heuristic that people can easily rely on to judge other forms. Dixon-Gottschild's work crucially reveals what has been omitted specifically in American modern dance history on the concert stage through the domination of Europeanist over Africanist aesthetics. But for dancers working outside of modern dance and the mainstream concert setting, this framework is insufficient because it does not fully address the issues of misunderstanding and devaluing that artists from other dance cultures all over the world—and from a variety of different racial and ethnic groups—experience. Many dancers do not work consistently within one or the other of these polarities. Instead, they intersect at various confluences and struggle for recognition and resources in many different ways. Anything outside of the bubble of the dominant brand appears to be unclear, uneducated, uncivilized, struggling to understand itself, and is consistently presented in the mainstream as illegible. Therefore, in this book, we consider the nuances that arise between these racially defined polarities to better understand what makes dance cultures and their associated identities so complex.

Another issue is that a binary framework marks Black dance in very particular ways but often leaves "White dance" largely unmarked, undiversified, and unexamined. There has been much conversation about the history of the term "Black dance" in the realm of American modern dance (e.g., Allen 1988; Dixon-Gottschild 1998, 2003; DeFrantz 2002; Amin 2011), but less so in the context of Black forms outside of modern dance. We aim to consider how such terms are deployed outside of concert dance spaces. We take specific issue with language that promotes the critical examination of some dance forms but not all (namely, the notion of a monolithic White form). Christopher Ugolo, one of Sinclair's mentors at the University of Benin, explained to him one day why he questioned the use of the terms "African dance" and "Black dance." Ugolo said, with some irritation, "If there is 'Black dance,' shouldn't there also be 'White dance'?"[3] He was referring to how the reclaimed identity of "Black dance" can also be used as a deterrent—one that prevents a dancer from having the agency to operate with dignity in any given space. The problem, as he described it, is in the naming of "Black dance" (or dance with any other racial or ethnic qualifier) as a way to quickly identify who can access the dance or who must be subjected to the tedious task of constantly justifying their practice to outsiders. So, if "Black dance" becomes such a brand marker, Ugolo asked, why then do we not also have a "White dance" so that we can have a clear comparison? Demarcating African dance or Black dance gives dancers in these categories their own space to operate in, but that distinction also gives dancers working in forms that can be described without racial, ethnic, or cultural qualifiers the leverage to move more fluidly and create more freely. Sinclair, for example, feels that in the United States he cannot break out of his identity as a Black African dancer, something that he never thought about at home in Nigeria. He now feels controlled by the expectations that accompany this particular identity. Those considered to be part of the mainstream by virtue of their skin color, on the other hand, can move more freely through confluent spaces because brand markers do not hold them in a fixed, static position.

In addition, if there is "Black dance" but no "White dance," then people who identify as participating in "White dance" are seen as acultural and neutral. In general, "White dance" calls to mind ballet and modern, but there are other "White dances" that are not referred to as such. Kate, for example, would not say that she does White dance because she does Irish dance specifically, which is described by a very distinct cultural marker. It has been made clear to her throughout her life that she does not navigate the dance field in the same way as practitioners of so-called "White dance"—i.e., ballet and modern. Practitioners of European folk forms like Irish dance are referred to by their national or regional marker, not an entire continent (unlike African dance), and they are not branded by their skin color. This erasure of Whiteness as a racial category is another effect of racism.[4] Being called a "White dancer" does not adequately describe her experience of being aware of her skin color within the dance field, while also not being able to relate to the mainstream dance forms associated with her racial group.

We fully recognize the need to distinguish dance forms by race, culture, ethnicity, nationality, and other social identities to recuperate lost histories and empower marginalized communities. For example, anthropologists Kurzwelly, Rapport, and Spiegel point to "active essentialism," or the ways that essentialist categorization, "whilst ultimately pernicious, sometimes manifests strategically in apparently worthy forms where its mobilisation contributes to efforts to overcome oppressive structures," as in situations like South African apartheid (2020, 66–69). In such cases in the context of dance, we must establish clear distinctions through language based on such categories to illustrate how inequities, injustices, and omissions have arisen over centuries. Having the agency to name dances and attach them to categories to describe the people who practice them is a big part of how dancers become empowered to live out their identities in practice and performance. But identification is not a linear process based on essentialist, socially constructed definitions. As José Esteban Muñoz explains, performances of "disidentification" work on and against "socially prescriptive patterns of identification" to redefine mainstream aesthetic codes and transform oppressive cultural structures from within (1999, 28). He describes disidentification as a strategy of resistance or survival for minoritarian subjects to "negotiate between fixed [identities] and the socially encoded roles available [to them]" that neither assimilate nor oppose the dominant identity (1999, 6). For many groups throughout the world, for example, re-appropriating derogatory terms that have been used to diminish them can be empowering and used as a form of resistance. We build on the theory of disidentification to account for migrations between identities and the contested borders that we are talking about, as well as the ability to occupy multiple, differential streams at once in confluent dance spaces.

Our challenge in co-writing this book has been to develop a discourse of cultural confluences in order to help us find common ground while considering our racial differences and examining them more deeply. Recent language and frameworks in the academic dance field suggest that the two of us are separated by an unbridgeable racial gap, but we know through our conversations that we share experiences of migration and displacement, nonetheless. Formulating language that considers our differences while also exploring our similarities is an empowering step forward in our field.

Language in dance scholarship and teaching

Both of us have encountered the issue of being asked to quote scholarly books and articles about the dances we practice and apply theories from mainstream dance and performance cultures to our own. There are far fewer books about our dance cultures than there are about more mainstream dances in the United States, and even where there are books written about the dance forms we practice, we still want to emphasize the importance of valuing actual embodied experience within a community. We believe that theory itself in dance does not only come from a textbook or in writings by Western scholars, but it arises directly from lived experience within communities. We need to rethink the many ways that embodied knowledge is created and represented within a wide variety of dance cultures around the world beyond spoken or written language.

Being asked to cite scholarship about our dance cultures written by outsiders demonstrates a certain suspicion of indigenous epistemologies outside of the mainstream. For example, during an on-campus interview for a faculty position at a college dance program, Sinclair was asked to teach a contemporary African dance class. One of his interviewers, who is prominent in the dance field, commented to him, "I wonder what the students are actually learning in your class." This person went on to challenge him to find out what books he had read about African dance and about dance in general, forgetting (or ignoring) the fact that he has a terminal degree in dance from a U.S. institution and that, more importantly, African dance history lives and manifests in the body—in *his* body. He was so stunned by the question and the way she wielded her power to intimidate him in the interview that he did not know how to respond, and he knew that she was not looking for a response. Ignoring the wealth of knowledge that resides within his practice and asking him to legitimize his knowledge of his own body and African cultures through "book reading" was offensive and humiliating. The interviewer's questions made his embodied experience insignificant by communicating her expectation that an African dance artist and scholar should read books about African dance written by foreigners to understand his craft. Much of the literature that does exist about African dance was written without a full understanding of the cultural context that exists within communities and has been used as a way to manipulate less elite dancers. Sinclair has also noticed how the language of oral tradition in his community has been influenced by academic language and, conversely, that academic language has used and continues to use tools from oral traditions. Borrowing language from oral traditions may mean that those oral traditions go unrecognized or uncredited. A major goal of this book (especially Chapter 5) is to point to the ways that we can recognize the value of embodied knowledge that arises directly from communities and use language that reflects indigenous epistemologies that are otherwise difficult to express or represent in mainstream academic frameworks.

In the dance field, we do more than just talk and write. We dance. To dance is to perform, partake in, and commit to a process of knowledge creation that invites participation. Dancers of all forms are challenged with the task of describing embodied knowledge in words, and it is difficult to write about dance or any kinesthetic experience. Physical movement speaks for itself in various ways, and spoken elements—and, in some forms, vocalizations through ululations, chants, or incantations that are non-syllabic or indistinct—also enhance dance practices. Some non-mainstream dance forms do not rely primarily on language for transmission, and learning happens through imitation, as described earlier, and embodied transmission of non-linguistic movement vocabularies. For example, in *Sensational Knowledge: Embodying Culture through Nihon Buyo Dance*, ethnomusicologist Tomie Hahn describes how *nihon buyo* dance from Japan is passed down through many different channels including tactioception (touch), smell, sound, and sight for embodied multi-sensory learning (2007). In the realm of percussive dance, Kate similarly notes the very distinct ways that dancers who make noise engage with movement, rhythm, and music such that sonic elements take precedence over the visual. In addition, teachers of many dance (and music) forms use vocables to accentuate their teaching, guiding the emphasis of the movement or keeping time with non-translatable sounds (e.g., "la," "ha," "dah," "dun," "boom," "dee," "shak," etc.).[5] These sounds, rhythms, and multi-sensory cues constitute a language of their own. We are specifically interested in the language of oral traditions—which, although it is commonly called "oral," is often more "kinesthetic" and embodied than it is oral or verbal. Our dance cultures rely on such traditions for transmission and continuity, and we find it difficult to articulate how to place value on practices that cannot be described in the language that is preferred by Western education systems.

As dance educators Crystal Davis and Jesse Phillips-Fein point out, there seems to be an assumption that Western dance language (i.e., from ballet and modern) serves any form and can replace language specific to any dance culture in the classroom (2018). We are not saying that none of this language can be used to describe our dance cultures. Rather, we believe it is limited and does not fully articulate all dance practices and the value they bring to the field. To cite one common example, a *plié* is a ballet term that refers to a bend in the knees, and we have heard colleagues describe the plié as a "neutral" and foundational movement in dance, especially to prepare for and land a jump. However, the training needed to do a plié is distinct from the training to bend the knees in, for example, African forms, just as a bend in the knee before and after jumping is avoided in Irish dance technique.[6] But in college dance classes, we have heard this term used to guide students through forms like hip-hop and African dances without distinguishing the plié in ballet from the mechanics of a knee bend or jump preparation in another form. This is just one example in which ballet terminology and the technical training that arises from it do not serve all forms.

Bringing non-mainstream dance forms into higher education is challenging. Students often arrive with the assumption that ballet and modern are "real dance," whereas anything else is "just for fun." Kate teaches a dance ethnography class in which students learn about a variety of dance cultures and they have numerous opportunities to work with guest instructors who are experts in their form. Her students get a taste of multiple forms to gain a broader understanding and appreciation for why people throughout the world dance—whether as joyful expression, sacred worship, or revolution and resistance. The "tasting menu" approach to dance risks becoming a survey-style introduction to many global forms without much context, but Kate foregrounds the ways that the local connects to the global. Throughout the course, students investigate how each dance style has its own distinct context and set of concerns and how common themes cut across many dances. She begins the semester by asking students to read Joann Kealiinohomoku's "Folk Dance" (1972), which challenges students' preconceptions about what "folk dance" is and sets the stage for them to begin questioning their assumptions when they first encounter an unfamiliar dance form. The course then guides them through this line of questioning as they develop research projects on a dance or movement culture of their choice. As one of her students said at the end of one semester, "Questioning causes you to frame your thoughts as though they are not the only way to think, but as simply one of the many ways to think." The willingness to question is key to challenging the language we rely on to talk about dance. If a term starts to feel too easy or overused, we reexamine it and ask if another term might be more appropriate.

As educators who teach dance forms from "other" cultures, cultural appropriation is a topic that comes up a lot. We have both been confronted with the idea that it is wrong to engage with cultures other than one's own. The perceived risk is that taking on the characteristics of a dance culture other than the one associated with one's own skin color, ethnicity, or nationality can be understood as appropriation. We have been met with resistance from students who are reluctant to, and in some cases fearful of, learning about other dance cultures because they are worried about saying or doing the wrong thing, or being accused of appropriation for participating in a culture that is not their own. This is especially difficult for White students in the United States, who often express to us that they do not have a culture. We have found that students are afraid to share their opinions and thoughts as they become more conscious of appropriation and "call out" or "cancel" culture, in which a person is accused of saying or doing something offensive. These are valid concerns, and we certainly want to avoid the harm that can be inflicted by insensitive or aggressive comments and actions. But we also believe there are ways to equip students in the classroom with the language and skills to participate in a variety of dance forms with respect and a curious attitude. Acknowledging and challenging the biases and assumptions that students come in with can help them engage in these difficult conversations. This paradigm shift helps us see the incredible amount of power language has on dance, from the ways we use words for movement instruction in the dance studio to the ways that words are weaponized in conversations. It is important to offer students a clear set of guiding principles and parameters on how language can be used in positive, uplifting ways instead of exclusionary, belittling ways.

One tactic that Sinclair uses in his college-level African dance classes is to ask his students, at the beginning of the semester, for their consent to teach them movements and patterns from African dance cultures. He asks, "Do I have your permission to give you this movement, to put this movement on your bodies? Understand that you will carry this in your bodies from now on." The idea is that, in learning new forms of movement, students will pick up new patterns—a new kinesthetic "language"—that will become imprinted on their bodies, and he guides them to learn a new way of moving in the world, understanding his culture from an embodied place. This question indicates Sinclair's awareness of the potential effects his teaching can have on his students, who are primarily trained in ballet and modern dance. These potential effects include the risk that some of the prejudice that he has experienced because he looks and moves a certain way will be passed on to them if they also start to move in those ways. Because of this experience and seeing how some of his students have been accused of appropriating African dance after incorporating elements from his class into their own creative work, asking for consent feels like the ethical thing to do.

Teaching dances that are traditionally practiced outside of a concert setting is often considered to be something that people just do "for fun," but the reality is that the ways we move and present ourselves through bodily postures and gestures in any setting are highly politicized in today's world. The idea of asking dance students for consent to imprint new movement patterns on them is revolutionary because it indicates just how powerful dance and movement training can be. The ethical responsibility of the instructor is to consider what the adoption of certain movement patterns means for an individual body—taking into consideration their racial, ethnic, national, and gender identities—and what the individual could potentially do with that movement. Similarly, fostering a healthy amount of doubt and questioning reminds us that categories, labels, and brand markers are fabricated and do not fully describe one's lived experience. It is a challenge to convey the seriousness of these issues while also emphasizing the value of dance as playful activity, as discussed in the following section.

Students in our classes have reported that, by being asked for their consent or asked to continually question what they think they know about a dance form, they feel a burden of responsibility, and they more fully grasp the power of movement. They are not just being invited into a space to imitate a couple of dance steps, nor are they being asked to simply talk about dance. They are asked to critically engage in a multi-layered process of cultural understanding. This process gives them the agency to perform and use the skills they learn in class to expand their range as movers and creators. Crucial to this pedagogy is the process of equipping students with more nuanced language to talk and think critically about what they are learning, as well as realize the need to go beyond language when studying dance. We have students from many different cultural backgrounds and racial and ethnic groups and, due to this pedagogy, many of our students have mentioned that they feel liberated, free, and heard in our classes. Some have even said that our classes have awakened in them a desire to travel and learn more about other cultures when, just a few months before, they were afraid of even talking about another culture. Through their embodied studies, they have discovered that dance is not necessarily about mastery of technique and being "good" from a technical standpoint, but that playfulness and questioning also constitute "serious" engagement with dance.

Dance as play

In this final section, we consider the meaning and connotations of the word "dance" itself as it is used in various movement cultures. Sinclair remembers a conversation he had in a choreography class in graduate school about the notion that dance is a universal concept. Everyone was shocked when he mentioned that there is no word like "dance" in his culture. In the Urhobo language, *Ekha* is an adjective loosely translated into English as "play," but it is also used when referring to dance, usually with other qualifiers like *Egbe*, which further qualifies what type of Ekha "play" it is. In the Urhobo cosmogony, *Ekha-egbe* would translate to something more meaningful, tangible, and valuable within the dramatization and performance of "dance" as an activity. Such play constitutes the ways that children learn to form relationships while imitating adults. For example, in the moonlight dance in Urhobo land, children play to learn how a fisherman navigates his boat and how crucial it is for the fisherman to catch fish to nourish his family. Children gather to sing, "Mamako mamako ovwera …. oye mamako," as they sit in a row on the ground, as if in a boat, paddling an invisible canoe. This dance is playful, but it is a dramatization of what adults do while fishing in the riverine area of Delta State. This dance—this play—carries with it valuable customs across generations.

How did Sinclair's people make this translation from play to dance in English? Was it influenced by the presence of Western scholarship on the form in which Western scholars separate dance from music and other cultural practices? Sinclair sees the lack of a word for "dance" in his local tongue as a sign that the practice of dance, as understood in a Western context, is not, in fact, a universal concept. That is, a Western understanding of dance is just one way to consider how the body moves expressively to music, rhythm, or even silence. Western scholarship has neglected the fact that societies that have existed on their own for centuries have generated their own understanding of movement, along with their own language to describe it.

According to Sinclair, there are a few reasons why his people do not have words for dance and other objects and activities associated with dancing. First, they may not recognize dance as a "valuable" activity in the sense that it is so fundamental to them (along with language and other social customs) that it almost goes unnoticed. Or maybe the concept of dance became more pronounced during nationalization and the formation of statehood and political identities during Nigeria's postcolonial era, when his community began to place economic value on dance, along with other cultural products, as it was bought and sold in the global market. It is difficult to put language to the value of something that is simply a part of life and not presented for monetary exchange or barter in the capitalist system. Is there a way to value something just because it is embedded in one's lifestyle? Can the process of creation be more valuable than the created product?

If dance is not "dance" in Sinclair's Urhobo community, then what is it? Should we try to define it at all? If the definition turns out to be completely different from what has been deemed to be the "right way" of understanding and presenting dance in our field, can there be room for such difference to thrive? Are we sure that there is, in fact, dance within every community in the world? Does everyone in the world have a sense of what it means to dance? Is there a reason why a culture would call the act of dancing "playing"?

Language comes into play in how people describe serious and meaningful practices and how they use terms meant to diminish a dance that they see as less rigorous. Problems arise when dance is simply referred to as "play" because it connotes a practice that is less serious or "just for fun." Western cosmology separates play from serious inquiry, ignoring the fact that play can intertwine many different aspects of cognition, learning, articulation, reflection, remembering, history, and ethics, especially when it comes to learning how to dance. In spaces where seriousness is valued over play, "serious" learning tools replace the playful social interactions that serve an important role in social development and cultural transmission in some communities, relegating dance as play to the margins of confluent spaces.

If dance is play, we also have to consider what kind of play it might be. We find examples of the verb "to play" itself having different connotations in some dance cultures. Is play a form of cultural interplay that can generate new embodied knowledge? As Johan Huizinga writes, play is "a free activity standing quite consciously outside 'ordinary' life as being 'not serious,' but at the same time absorbing the player intensely and utterly" (1998, 13). The concept of "serious play" has been explored by scholars such as Victor Turner (1986) and Roberto Da Matta (1984, 1991) in the specific context of spatial configurations of ritual play during Brazilian carnival.[7] Building on this theory, Kate has noted in her studies of Brazilian capoeira and frevo that the verbs *jogar* and *brincar* are used to differentiate the kind of play that practitioners of each form engage in (Spanos 2019). Frevo developed from capoeira during street carnivals in northeastern Brazil in the late nineteenth century, a time when people from many social groups and classes congregated in the streets, resulting in a different kind of playful interaction between practitioners than in capoeira. In modern capoeira, two players or opponents *jogam* (play) what is referred to as a "game" in the center of the *roda* (the circular formation in which the game takes place), and they generally abide by certain rules and etiquette. In frevo, practitioners *brincam*, which is more akin to "child's play" and connotes a ludic practice that is more about having undirected, pleasurable fun than it is about engaging in a ritualized game or competition between two people. As a result of these different connotations of play, these dances look entirely different from the outside, even though they share similar origins and philosophies and circulate in a shared confluent space. If dance is play, we must also consider what kind of play it is.

There is a tendency to dismiss certain dance cultures because they are "all fun and games," but on the other side of this issue is the tendency for outsiders to dismiss unfamiliar dance forms by saying that they are too "hard." In the latter case, one must be highly specialized and trained to dance the form—or simply be "born with it." Both Kate and Sinclair have experienced this attitude in dealing with students and other dance colleagues who insist that their dance practices are too difficult to learn. While this could be seen, and may often be meant, as a compliment (who doesn't want to be told that their dancing is very impressive?), this kind of comment is another example of how language can be used to exclude and justify why certain dance cultures should not be widely taught. These forms are exoticized to the extent that outsiders believe they cannot and should not participate. Again, we have encountered many people who are afraid of participating in our forms for fear of being accused of cultural appropriation. We know, however, that many of the dance cultures that we talk about in this book are inherently participatory and community-based, even if styles or branches of these forms have developed that are more virtuosic and showier. Can we adapt our language to express that a dance culture is somewhere between "all fun and games" and "too hard"? Again, we find ourselves trapped within an either/or binary and stuck in alternating categories of good, bad, too good, or not good enough.

Conclusion

In this chapter, we have examined the language used in mainstream academic and professional dance spaces to expand on our framework of cultural confluences, which encapsulates the nonlinear ways that dancers migrate through various spaces. Brand markers defined by race, ethnicity, geographic location, or nationality highlight the relationship between mainstream values and the marketplace in the dance field. We have explored how dances that rely more on kinesthetic imitation than on codified terminology are seen as less legible, and thus less valuable, and how this plays out in the classroom and academic work.

Our examination of dance as play—a fully embodied and serious practice—leads into the following chapter about aesthetic value and how judgments are formed about what makes "good" and "bad" dance. Building on what dance in everyday life means, we consider definitions of "art" and the commodification of aesthetic value in dance. We build on this discussion about language to consider how critical engagement with a variety of aesthetic systems is a crucial part of promoting diversity, equity, and inclusion in our field.

Notes

1 Internet memes connect to Dawkins' original definition of a meme in the sense that they represent the viral replication and mutation of ideas or practices (Solon 2013). But they differ in the sense that Internet memes are traceable by digital footprint, whereas embodied memes are not (Coscia 2013).
2 It is also worth noting the ways that words like "verticality" and "uprightness" related to posture in Western aesthetics have been politicized throughout history, including the implications this language has for determining able-bodiedness in modern culture (Gilman 2018).
3 Thomas DeFrantz also asks why there is no category of "White dance" in *Dancing Many Drums: Excavations in African American Dance*, 2002, 3–35.
4 For more on the erasure and "coloring" of Whiteness in culture and performance, see Dyer (1997), Rasmussen et al. (2001), Garner (2007), Bayor (2009), and Carpenter (2014).
5 For more about the meaning of "nonsense" syllables in music, see Hughes (2000) and Mullins (2014).
6 In *Butting Out*, Ananya Chatterjea writes about the concept of a "'perfectly' executed plié" in the work of choreographer Jawole Willa Jo Zollar, "rewriting the rules of linear alignment" to reflect "swaying hips and curving butt" in African diasporic dance (2004, 190). Chatterjea also analyzes the differences between a "plié" and a "knee bend" in classical Indian dance through the work of choreographer Chandralekha.
7 Other writings about dance performance and play in African and Caribbean cultures include, for example, Drewal (1991), Okagbue (1997, 2007, 2021), and Nicholls (2012).

References

Allen, Zita. 1988. "What Is Black Dance?" In *The Black Tradition in Modern Dance*, edited by Gerald E. Myers, 22–3, American Dance Festival Booklet.
Amin, Takiyah Nur. 2011. "A Terminology of Difference: Making the Case for Black Dance in the 21st Century and Beyond." *The Journal of Pan-African Studies* 4 (6): 7–15.
Bannerman, Henrietta. 2014. "Is Dance a Language? Movement, Meaning and Communication." *Dance Research: The Journal of the Society for Dance Research* 32 (1): 65–80.
Bayor, Ronald H. 2009. "Another Look at 'Whiteness': The Persistence of Ethnicity in American Life." *Journal of American Ethnic History* 29: 13–30.
Blackmore, Susan J. 1999. *The Meme Machine*. Oxford, UK: Oxford University Press.
Boast, Robin. 2011. "Neocolonial Collaboration: Museum as Contact Zone Revisited." *Museum Anthropology* 34 (1): 56–70. https://doi.org/10.1111/j.1548-1379.2010.01107.x.

Carpenter, Faedra Chatard. 2014. *Coloring Whiteness: Acts of Critique in Black Performance*. Theater: Theory/Text/Performance. Ann Arbor, MI: University of Michigan Press.

Chatterjea, Ananya. 2004. *Butting Out: Reading Resistive Choreographies Through Works by Jawole Willa Jo Zollar and Chandralekha*. Middletown, CT: Wesleyan University Press.

Copeland, Roger, and Marshall Cohen. 1983. *What Is Dance?: Readings in Theory and Criticism*. Oxford, UK: Oxford University Press.

Coscia, Michele. 2013. "Competition and Success in the Meme Pool: A Case Study on Quickmeme.com." http://arxiv.org/abs/1304.1712.

Da Matta, Roberto. 1984. "Carnival in Multiple Planes." In *Rite, Drama, Festival, Spectacle: Rehearsals Toward a Critical Performance*, edited by John J. MacAloon, 208–39. Philadelphia, PA: Institute for the Study of Human Issues.

———. 1991. *Carnivals, Rogues, and Heroes: An Interpretation of the Brazilian Dilemma*. Notre Dame: University of Notre Dame Press.

Davis, Crystal U., and Jesse Phillips-Fein. 2018. "Tendus and Tenancy: Black Dancers and the White Landscape of Dance Education." In *The Palgrave Handbook of Race and the Arts in Education*, edited by Amelia M. Kraehe, Rubén A. Gaztambide-Fernández, and B. Stephen Carpenter II, 571–84. Cham, Switzerland: Palgrave Macmillan.

DeFrantz, Thomas F. 2002. *Dancing Many Drums: Excavations in African American Dance*. Madison, WI: University of Wisconsin Press.

Dixon-Gottschild, Brenda. 1998. *Digging the Africanist Presence in American Performance: Dance and Other Contexts*. Westport, CT: Praeger Publishers.

———. 2003. *The Black Dancing Body: A Geography from Coon to Cool*. New York, NY: Palgrave Macmillan.

Drewal, Margaret Thompson. 1991. *Yoruba Ritual: Performers, Play, Agency*. Bloomington, IN: Indiana University Press.

Dyer, Richard. 1997. "The Matter of Whiteness." In *White: Essays on Race and Culture*, 1–40. London, UK: Routledge.

Foley, Catherine E. 2012. *Irish Traditional Step Dancing in North Kerry: A Contextual and Structural Analysis*. Listowel: North Kerry Literary Trust.

Foster, Susan Leigh. 1986. *Reading Dancing: Bodies and Subjects in Contemporary American Dance*. Berkeley, CA: University of California Press.

———. 2019. *Valuing Dance: Commodities and Gifts in Motion*. New York, NY: Oxford University Press. https://doi.org/10.1093/oso/9780190933975.001.0001.

Garner, Steven. 2007. "How the Irish Became White (Again)." In *Whiteness: An Introduction*, 120–35. London, UK: Routledge.

Gilman, Sander L. 2018. *Stand up Straight!: A History of Posture*. London, UK: Reaktion Books.

Hahn, Tomie. 2007. *Sensational Knowledge: Embodying Culture Through Japanese Dance*. Middletown, CT: Wesleyan University Press.

Hanna, Judith Lynne. 1987. *To Dance Is Human: A Theory of Nonverbal Communication*. Chicago, IL: University of Chicago Press.

Hughes, David W. 2000. "No Nonsense: The Logic and Power of Acoustic-iconic Mnemonic Systems." *British Journal of Ethnomusicology* 9 (2): 93–120. https://doi.org/10.1080/09681220008567302.

Huizinga, Johan. 1998. *Homo Ludens: A Study of the Play-Element in Culture*. Reprint of the 1949 edition. 3. London, UK: Routledge.

Kaeppler, Adrienne L. 1972. "Method and Theory in Analyzing Dance Structure with an Analysis of Tongan Dance." *Ethnomusicology* 16: 173–217.

Kealiinohomoku, Joann Wheeler. 1972. "Folk Dance." In *Folklore & Folklife: An Introduction*, edited by Richard M. Dorson. Chicago, IL: University of Chicago Press.

Keller, Kevin Lane, and Donald R. Lehmann. 2006. "Brands and Branding: Research Findings and Future Priorities." *Marketing Science* 25 (6): 740–59. https://doi.org/10.1287/mksc.1050.0153.

Kurzwelly, Jonatan, Nigel Rapport, and Andrew Spiegel. 2020. "Encountering, Explaining and Refuting Essentialism." *Anthropology Southern Africa* 43 (April): 65–81. https://doi.org/10.1080/23323256.2020.1780141.

Mullins, Catherine. 2014. "Blah, Blah, Blah: Making Sense of Nonsense in Irish Vocal Music." *Musical Offerings* 5 (2): 87–117. https://doi.org/10.15385/jmo.2014.5.2.2.

Muñoz, José Esteban. 1999. "Performing Disidentifications." In *Disidentifications: Queers of Color and the Performance of Politics*, 1–34. Minneapolis, MN: University of Minnesota Press.

Nicholls, Robert. 2012. *The Jumbies' Playing Ground: Old World Influence on Afro-Creole Masquerades in the Eastern Caribbean*. Jackson, MS: University Press of Mississippi.

Okagbue, Osita. 1997. "When the Dead Return: Play and Seriousness in African Masked Performances." *South African Theatre Journal* 11 (1–2): 89–107.

———. 2007. *African Theatres and Performances*. Theatres of the World. London, UK: Routledge.

———. 2021. "Playing with Our Ancestors: Culture and Communal Memory in Igbo Masquerade Theatre." *African Performance Review* 11 (1).

Pratt, Mary Louise. 1991. "Arts of the Contact Zone." *Profession*, 33–40.

Preston-Dunlop, Valerie. 1995. *Dance Words*. Choreography and Dance Studies. Chur, Switzerland: Harwood Academic Publishers.

Rasmussen, Birgit Brander, Eric Klinenberg, Irene J. Nexica, and Matt Wray, eds. 2001. *The Making and Unmaking of Whiteness*. Durham, NC: Duke University Press.

Royce, Anya Peterson. 1977. *The Anthropology of Dance*. Bloomington, IN: Indiana University Press.

Savigliano, Marta. 2009. "Worlding Dance and Dancing Out There in the World." In *Worlding Dance*, edited by Susan Leigh Foster, 163–90. Basingstoke, NY: Palgrave Macmillan.

Sklar, Deidre. 1991. "Five Premises for a Culturally Sensitive Approach to Dance." In *Moving History/Dancing Cultures: A Dance History Reader*, edited by Ann Dils and Ann Cooper Albright, 30–3. Middletown, CT: Wesleyan University Press.

Solon, Olivia. 2013. "Richard Dawkins on the Internet's Hijacking of the Word 'Meme.'" Wired UK. July 9, 2013. https://www.wired.co.uk/article/richard-dawkins-memes.

Spanos, Kathleen A. 2019. "A Dance of Resistance from Recife, Brazil: Carnivalesque Improvisation in Frevo." *Dance Research Journal* 51 (3): 28–46. https://doi.org/10.1017/S0149767719000305.

Turner, Victor. 1986. "Carnival in Rio: Dionysian Drama in an Industrializing Society." In *The Anthropology of Performance*, 103–24. New York, NY: PAJ Publications.

Van Ede, Yolanda. 2014. "Japanized Flamenco: Sensory Shifts in a Transcultural Relocation of a Dance Genre." *Journal of Dance & Somatic Practices* 6 (1): 61–74. https://doi.org/10.1386/jdsp.6.1.61_1.

Williams, Drid. 1979. "The Human Action Sign and Semasiology." *Dance Research Annual* 10: 39–64.

———. 1999. "Messages, Meaning and the Moving Body." *Visual Anthropology* 12 (1): 87–97. https://doi.org/10.1080/08949468.1999.9966768.

2 Critical engagement with aesthetic systems in dance

In this chapter, we examine how aesthetic values are configured, trained, and experienced in different dance cultures. We build on our framework of cultural confluences by looking at how distinct aesthetic systems in dance clash and/or feed into each other. As dance educator Crystal Davis notes, both implicit and explicit biases establish systemic power imbalances in dance spaces based on the aesthetic values of an individual or institution (2022). In our work, we first consider the role of aesthetics in understanding what dance does for us and what we can do with dance. We then expand on our examination of language from the previous chapter to question whether all cultural movement practices should be called "dance" and "art," or whether we need different terminology when considering concert stage performances versus community practices. In so doing, we resist aesthetic categories that appeal to the global display, consumption, and commodification of marginalized dance cultures merely as entertainment or curiosities. We are especially concerned with how cultural biases within the Western mainstream establish assumptions about what is and is not art. We put pressure on the notion of "good" and "bad" in dance, instead asking whether there is room for different aesthetic systems to coexist in our field.

This chapter introduces our use of interludes to provide more insight into how our personal experiences shape the way we grapple with aesthetic questions in our lives as dancers and educators. Each vignette reflects how we think about value in the dance cultures we come from and study in terms of the "intellect" of the body, whose aesthetics belong to whom, building cross-cultural and interpersonal empathy through kinesthetic exploration, and what aesthetic value feels like in the body.

What does dance do for us?

In questioning what makes dance "good," we first turn our examination to the relational, behavioral, and affective dimensions of dance cultures to emphasize the ways that value is shaped in confluent spaces. We examine the "good" that we can do with dance through our cultural encounters, as well as the "good" that dance does for us as practitioners. We believe that dance puts our bodies in a position to act and respond in culturally specific ways, learned through a combination of aesthetic movement training and social relations.

DOI: 10.4324/9781003231226-3

What value does dance bring to our lives? One commonly held perspective is that dance and the arts make us more empathetic, support mental and emotional health, cultivate civilization, and transform society in positive ways. However, education scholar Rubén Gaztambide-Fernández (2020) argues that, in fact, we do things *through* the arts. For him, the arts are not inherently "good." Their value depends on the agents—the people—who create and practice them, and people can do good or bad with the arts. He argues that the perspective that the arts "do things" for us comes from a Eurocentric understanding of culture. He traces this perspective back to Enlightenment ideas about how the arts "save" the "Other" and make them more "cultured" or "cultivated," and how this generates the understanding that the arts are valuable for their alleged ability to make us better, more coherent, rational, and productive human beings (Gaztambide-Fernández et al. 2018, 2020). The issue is that this "rhetoric of effects," as he calls it, creates the expectation that the arts be used to achieve a desired outcome and that we must justify our participation in them as though the arts exist outside of daily life. He is concerned with discourse about how the arts "foster," "promote," and "help," which frames creative practice from an instrumentalist approach, based on its power to transform or cultivate a person (2020, 7–10). He further cautions against the assumption that everything can be assimilated into Western ideas of what art is.

Gaztambide-Fernández proposes an examination of the "affective order" of the arts, which draws attention away from the Western aesthetic notion that an "artifact" is separate from its social order, and instead attends to the "structures of feeling" that arise from social interactions within a community. He differentiates between processes of cultural production that achieve "desired and predictable effects" versus the "affects" of creative practice, or the modes of being, making, and becoming in the world that arise from sensory, emotional, and embodied encounters with other human beings (2020, 18–19). This idea relates to the notion of kinesthetic empathy, or the ability to connect with other humans and bridge the distance between social environments through movement and affect (Reynolds and Reason 2012). In the context of cultural confluences, we see this emphasis on affect and empathy take shape in the ways that culturally defined aesthetic values arise from encounters and intersubjectivities within shared spaces. Attending to the "affects" of dance rather than its "effects" broadens our conversations about forms that thrive in community settings and helps us envision change in how dance forms are valued in mainstream Western spaces.

We also believe, however, that in dance specifically, embodied training and performing certain stylized movements can "do good things" for us. That is, dance can put one's body in a position to act in culturally specific ways. For us, this is what embodied knowledge is all about—as you engage with a new dance culture, you begin to see and experience the world and your own body in new ways. As exemplified in the interludes written by both of us throughout this chapter, we believe that the lessons learned by engaging with different dance aesthetics can also change a person. The caveat here is that observing dance from the outside is not enough. We must engage in learning and embodying these values from the inside, which can be difficult and often physically and emotionally uncomfortable. We should become comfortable with the idea that dance, when activated within our bodies along with other streams of embodied knowledge, becomes something more than we may have envisioned for ourselves when we set out on the process of learning a new way to move.

Dance does something to us—calling us to behave in a certain way based on specific cultural cues. Certainly, we have the agency to do good or bad with the knowledge we gain through the arts, as Gaztambide-Fernández suggests, but we should also consider what dance does for us by literally putting our bodies in position to behave in particular ways. We can think about agency in dance in the context of cultural historian Robin Bernstein's theory of "dances with things," which she uses to describe how material artifacts like books and dolls have been racialized throughout American history. She argues that "things" (as distinct from simple "objects") are performative in the sense that they constitute action. She says, "Things script meaningful bodily movements, and these citational movements think the otherwise unthinkable," adding, "Things are not alive, but people 'behave,' as W. J. T. Mitchell notes, 'as if works of art had minds of their own, as if images had a power to influence human beings, demanding things from us, persuading, seducing, and leading us astray'" (2009, 70).

Drawing on Louis Althusser's theory of how ideological values are internalized, Bernstein argues that a person engaging with a "scriptive thing" is interpellated to act in a certain way. This interpellation does not mean that the person lacks agency with regard to the "scriptive thing," but, as Bernstein notes, "agency, intention, and racial subjectivation co-emerge through everyday physical encounters with the material world" (2009, 68–69). In dance, the "scriptive thing" could literally be an article of clothing, a prop, or another accessory or body extension that compels the dancer to do something or move in a particular way. But we also add that dance itself, as a full system of cultural knowledge production, prompts a dancer to feel a certain way while moving—so we believe that the dance itself, too, could be a "scriptive thing." That is, both material and immaterial "things" can affect people, encouraging them to physically and psychologically behave in ways that are scripted through the dance. (We expand on this idea in the context of archival documentation of dance cultures in Chapter 5.)

To take one example of how dance behaviors are "scripted" in culturally defined spaces, Kate remembers the first time she went to a Brazilian samba event, around 2014 in Washington, D.C. She enjoyed the music and tried to pick up some of the samba steps, but she also remembers thinking afterward that she felt she was missing something. That is, she was missing the cultural knowledge that would allow her to fully appreciate the event. The samba rhythms did not "call" her to behave in a particular way, but she knew enough about other dance cultures to realize that there were cues that she was not picking up on. She knew the "thing" was there but didn't know how to respond to it or even recognize it. After a few months of consistently attending samba events, she ended up at a party at a Brazilian family's home and was struck by the ways that everyone participated in the *roda de samba* (like a samba jam session). Sitting in different spots around the living room, everyone started singing or pulling up lyrics on their mobile phones, and the older ladies danced a little samba in the corner. In this moment, it clicked for Kate that samba in this context was about joy, connection, and singing and dancing with family and friends, all in the midst of food and conversation. In particular, she noted some specific behavioral cues in terms of how people interacted with each other, when and how they participated in the music, and how the dancing was not something done for show but for pleasure, as though there was no choice but to participate. The music was a sort of "call to action" that everyone who understood those cues organized themselves around.

In its intangibility and immateriality, both of us see dance as absent until it is performed. Dance is a thing that is "out there" waiting for us to engage with it. To engage more fully, we feel that we experience a form of disembodiment and then re-embodiment in the process of learning a dance, such that we must mentally dissociate in order to make our bodies more receptive to adapting to new postures and gestures. The dance cultures that we participate in emphasize community connection and collective knowledge over self-conscious exploration. This runs counter to what is taught, for example, in somatic methodologies in which the individual, intellectual mind is emphasized. To allow this connection to take place, one must release the idea of engaging through rationality and instead tune into the body intellect that breaks down self-consciousness and allows for collective community expression. An example of this process happens during carnival, a time when individuality is set aside in favor of the power of the collective[1] in dance, music, and celebration. This, for us, is what the idea of confluences is about: learning, sharing, and experiencing the cultures that stream through our bodies and connect us with other bodies in the process.

Considering Gaztambide-Fernández's examination of arts that we do things with and Bernstein's notion of dancing with "things" in conjunction, we have to ask: Is the dance the thing, or is it the body? Within our culturally defined aesthetic systems, are we judging the body or the dance, or both at the same time? In aesthetic judgments of dance, we see three separate phenomena converge: (1) dance as an entity that is absent until it is actually embodied and performed; (2) the presence of the physical body, which performs the dance; and (3) the aesthetic system, which arises from ever-changing relations between performers, observers, critics, teachers, culture bearers, community members, and more. The dancing body is judged as all three of these elements come together, and judgments become increasingly complex in confluent spaces in which different aesthetic systems circulate. In such spaces, all would ideally be able to navigate more than one aesthetic system and understand how something could be valued in one culture but not in another without bias or judgment. Thus, in this chapter, we propose a total awareness of cultural confluences in the body when considering aesthetics in dance.

***

Interlude by Kate: The body is everything[2]

O corpo é tudo—the body is everything.

My teacher Fábio Soares da Silva repeated this phrase during each of our *cavalo marinho* classes when I was studying dance in Recife, Brazil in 2018. *Cavalo marinho* is a cultural practice performed in Brazil's northeastern state of Pernambuco, traditionally around Christmastime, that involves music, dance, and storytelling. It is practiced in the Zona da Mata, a rural region where communities subsist on sugarcane farming, which is physically demanding work. Soares is from a town in this region called Condado, but he moved to the state's capital, Recife, to become an independent dance artist. Everything that Soares taught us in the class started from the inside out, *de dentro pra fora*. Although we danced in a studio with marley floors, mirrors, and high ceilings in an urban area, he brought the feeling of Condado's dusty, narrow streets to us. We learned five steps in as many months, but we went deep into the nuances of those steps. I arrived early to classes and stayed late to listen to him talk about his family and his community, as well as the discrimination they face as poor, rural, Black/Indigenous people in the Zona da Mata.

He opened every class with the reminder, "Vai morrer—you're gonna die." He did not say this because he thought the dance was particularly hard, but because, "A gente é fraco—we are weak. We have been persecuted and we are going to die" (personal communication with Spanos, May 24, 2018). He explained that the steps were "simple," but I found them difficult and exhausting. During practice, he wanted us to feel that urgent, almost hopeless feeling of living a life that has been threatened by colonial violence for centuries. I knew that, as an outsider, I could not fully embody that feeling, but his words prompted me to sense the weight of such trauma in my body. I felt the soles of my feet pounding the ground and the skin on my toes burning from the friction. I had to lean my body forward, like that of someone who worked in the sugarcane fields all day, even though I had no idea what that work entailed—physically, emotionally, or politically. I mimicked his slight tilt of the head. I struggled through staggered weight shifts, crossing my legs over not too much and not too little, dropping my heel at just the right moment. Even when I was told to keep a natural posture and "do nothing," it became clear that my baseline of "nothing" was incorrect. I felt a certain hardness take over my body during these classes. Through practice, I felt myself connecting to and empathizing with a community that I had never met. Even though I had (and still have) much to learn about *cavalo marinho* and its music, characters, and stories, I was inspired by Soares' ability to instill so much of his community knowledge into us—not just through his words, but through the body. As he said, "O corpo é tudo, the body is everything." And not just the individual body, but the *corpo comunitário*, the collective body.

I first saw *cavalo marinho* in a video on Facebook a few months before I went to Recife. I was immediately drawn to it. I saw a *roda* ("wheel" or circular formation) of dancers and a *banco* (bench) of musicians that looked and sounded distantly familiar. Given my own cultural orientation, I thought that *cavalo marinho's rabeca* instrument looked and sounded much like the fiddle in American "old-time" music. To me, the footwork vaguely looked like Appalachian flatfooting. Old-time music and flatfooting are forms that arise from the confluence of African, Native American, and Scots Irish cultural encounters in the United States, and I wondered about the possibility of a parallel situation with regard to African, Indigenous, and European cultural influences in Brazil. At the same time, however, I could see that *cavalo marinho* involved many more elements that I did not recognize, like elaborate stories, characters, and jokes that were beyond my comprehension. When I started taking classes, *cavalo marinho* seemed to come from a world that I could only peek into under the careful guidance of my teacher. I understood that my experience with this dance was not through direct contact with the community itself—although Soares did take us to an event in his hometown of Condado one night. Instead, my experience took place primarily in a studio with one member of that community.

As I reflect on my experience learning about this dance, I think about what Soares taught me about embodied knowledge transmission, danced aesthetics, and indigenous epistemologies. His classes expanded my ideas about what pedagogy could look like in the context of an aesthetic system other than the one I was accustomed to. He guided us through exercises that prompted me to reflect on how body knowledge is transmitted within the community and how it is shared with outsiders in ways that demand respect. He insisted that one cannot attain the overall energy without studying the nuances of the steps. The steps themselves are entrenched in ritual and the details of *how* one performs them are crucial. Footwork from different traditions—even traditions from the same geographic region—may seem similar, but aesthetic subtleties of posture, rhythm, and energy are unique. Any variation makes the dance something else and may render the ritual invalid. In *cavalo marinho* classes, I wanted to shed my own ingrained bodily habits to see how deep my kinesthetic empathy could go. Even though I found some of the gestural footwork to be similar to Irish dance footwork, the dynamic energy, posture, and flow are entirely different from my vertical, upright tendencies, so I had to avoid reverting to my default technique. As Soares repeated, we could not let the movement become *outra coisa*, or something else.

Some of the most difficult exercises for me in Soares' classes were the interactions required by *cavalo marinho's mergulhão* (locally called the *magui*). The *mergulhão*, or "dive," happens in a *roda* formation. One person enters the circle and "calls" another person by grabbing their arm or just making eye contact; that person calls in another person and the process continues. Sometimes the call involves a kick or a *rasteira* ("sweep") that is reminiscent of an attack in capoeira, but one crucial difference is that each encounter lasts just a couple of seconds, and each call does not receive a direct response. As soon as you are called, you immediately choose someone else to call, so moments of connection pass in an instant. He also taught some steps from *maracatu rural*, another tradition from the Zona da Mata (distinct from *maracatu nação*, also from Pernambuco) that, among many distinct elements with deep significance, also involves a fight/dance/game between two *caboclos de lança*, or warrior figures connected to the *orixá* Ogum. I was reminded of capoeira in the *caboclo de lança* games, except that these interactions felt much slower. Soares directed us to skulk around our partner suspiciously while holding long wooden sticks called *guiadas*, only to interrupt the tension every so often with playful *giros* or spins that were meant to deflect or distract. Quick jabs kept us on guard. We also played with *o empurrão*—in which we pushed or shoved each other off balance in order to feel more weight and resistance as we fought to keep moving forward. These exercises were difficult for me because they required a very different type of interaction with my classmates than I was used to. I was often unsure if I should laugh or be afraid, and I felt the tension of the serious and the playful converging in my body. I understood this uncertainty to be the point of the exercise. I was learning to enjoy the game but to also watch my back at all times.

"O corpo é tudo" is a decolonial proposition. It challenges the ways we think about aesthetics as the elevated, intellectual significance ascribed to art by experts rather than something that is already embedded in cultural practice. This disruption becomes apparent in the movement of individual and communal bodies. Through "o corpo é tudo," we resist the Western notion that the mind is superior to the body. Sociologist Jessé Souza describes the history of this hierarchy in the construction of morality in middle-class Brazil, which he traces back to the opposition between the body and the spirit in European Christianity. In this often racialized and gendered moral system, the body is seen as "animalistic" and inferior, and the mind or the spirit as an elevated state of being (2018, 24–77). In improvisational or interactive practices like the Brazilian movement forms I have studied, the notion of the body as mind becomes apparent in the spontaneous dialogue between practitioners in the *roda*. Within Brazilian and many other African diasporic forms, a *roda*-like space is a common element, but each form uses the circle for a different purpose according to different rules of engagement. To understand and participate appropriately, one must be attuned to the cultural cues of that community. The body has an intellect of its own that "speaks" as it moves.

Soares insisted that "o corpo é tudo," but he also repeated, "Além de tudo, é dança" ("Besides all that, it's dance"), suggesting that all the history and details surrounding the dance were beside the point because it is, in the end, just a dance, just a part of life, and maybe we do not always need to take it so seriously. He used the word "dance" in a way that made the practice seem less important. But, in so doing, he also made the case for how integral it is to life in the Zona da Mata, elevating it beyond "just dance." In his culture and many others, nothing is more important than life. And if dance is life, it is more important than anything else we could possibly equate it to. From this perspective, the realm of aesthetic judgments is not even close to being able to describe what dance is meant to achieve for people who value their community life and the dances in it.

***

Art, culture, and aesthetics in confluent spaces

One of the biggest problems with using language like "art," "performance," and even "dance," to describe community traditions is that language itself has been used as a weapon in colonization, forcing not only dominant languages onto colonized communities but also the ideologies and epistemologies carried by language. Like Soares in the preceding vignette, some dancers take their practice seriously but insist that what they do is not art but just "everyday life." For Soares, separating "art" from life is a form of *escravidão do corpo*, or "enslavement of the body"

(ConVIDA! – Conversa Cabôca Com Joab Jó [PE] 2020). In a conversation with Kate, he explained that, for him, *cavalo marinho* is actually not "art" or "dance," neither "popular culture" nor "performance." These are words that outsiders use (May 24, 2018). He is concerned about *cavalo marinho's* rise in popularity within urban Recife, where it is transposed into performance settings by people who do not necessarily understand where the form comes from or what purpose it serves in his community. This transposition results in, for example, cutting the length of the event from eight or nine hours down to one, which in turn results in cutting out characters, storylines, and opportunities for jokes and social commentary intended for insiders with intimate knowledge of the community. The commodification of *cavalo marinho* as an "art form" to be enjoyed as entertainment is, for him, far from the ritual that he knows from his home village. Within the community, *cavalo marinho* practitioners do not "perform" for others, nor do they need to explain its value. Rather, they do it for themselves. The "training," so to speak, is built into everyday community life.

It is important to explain that both of us struggle with the term "everyday life" in the context of aesthetic value because it calls to mind something that is less serious and not valuable. First, an "everyday" practice is not necessarily a commonplace activity that is everywhere or that everyone can do. It does not mean that everyone goes around dancing or singing all the time. But it does refer to practices that are more embedded in community life with little or no separation between practitioners and spectators. The practice's value arises from these social relations. Second, we see a difference between valuing something that is made to be "art" (something considered "new" and uniquely "innovative") as opposed to that which already exists and is practiced by many. Many traditional communities put great emphasis on "carrying culture," which involves representing the culture and sustaining its communal practice, rather than creating it anew and being recognized as its "creator." In mainstream Western culture, we see that in order for a dance to be valued as art, it often has to be seen as innovative and then promoted so that people buy into it. This is different from Nigerian dance cultures or Brazilian *cavalo marinho*, for example, where the practice is part of people's lives, and they carry it on without the need to buy it as something separate from or supplemental to life. In addition, because of this Western perspective, tradition bearers from these cultures may not see themselves as artists and creators because the culture has been so deeply embedded in their community for many generations. But they carry valuable embodied knowledge. We expand on these ideas in Chapters 4 and 5 about how dancers from non-mainstream forms create, transmit, archive, and remember their dances.

In our own dance communities, both of us have heard much disagreement about whether dance can be called art if it is part of "everyday culture" and not performed on stage. Similarly, whether or not a dancer is an "artist" is called into question if they do not pursue their practice as a profession or life vocation. For some traditional dancers, the idea of "art" connotes a commodity to be sold in a local, regional, or global market, rather than a living practice, and they avoid such commodification in order to remain "authentic" to the form as it is practiced in the community. This distrust of art as a concept suggests a sort of inverted value system from the Western one, in which their practice is more than "just art" or "just dance" because it pervades cultural life. From this perspective, calling something art requires separating it from culture, putting it up on a pedestal, and presenting it on stage, in a museum, or in another setting outside of the community from which it comes. For these practitioners, such a separation means cutting off the dance from everything that makes it meaningful.

The differentiation between art and culture also depends on the local translation of these terms. For example, Sinclair experienced some dissonance when he came to the United States because, in his community in Nigeria, they tend to deal with the "cultural" with the same seriousness as the West considers "art." In primary schools, so-called "cultural dance" is considered "real dance," meaning a more serious expression of cultural knowledge and talent, while "art" is less serious and more like craft-making and make-believe. In Nigeria, very few are recognized as being gifted enough to drum, dance, and sing at community events. The language of colonization, however, has turned this around when considering African dance in the United States, resulting in the presentation of African dance as "cultural" by Western standards, meaning that it is treated as less serious than "art."

On the other side of this debate, we hear arguments that embracing one's practice as an art form—calling it "art" in a Western sense—is important to lending legitimacy to forms that have been marginalized. Doing so opens doors for other dancers from non-mainstream forms to expand what can be defined and accepted as art in academia and professional dance spaces. This approach requires a lot of work to redefine expectations about what dance is and should be in these spaces. Can we reconfigure this definition so that someone like Soares would be comfortable calling *cavalo marinho* an art form, or is the term already too loaded? When we call for a reconfiguration of the expectations that people have about dance, we are not talking about the expectations of people who already consider their cultural practices to have artistic merit. We are talking about gatekeepers who say that they don't. The work of redefining and proving aesthetic value is not up to those whose work has already been marginalized. It is up to those who have marginalized them. That said, our purpose here is to explore the ways that we can articulate the value that such forms bring to the field. This is challenging because so much of the valorization process comes through one's embodied, unspoken experience with the culture. The body is everything. The experience of dancing may seem solely physical and emotional until we recognize how embodiment and intellectual engagement can occur simultaneously and unconsciously.

We have asked ourselves: in our respective dance cultures, do we think we are sharing art or culture—or both? When we have been questioned in the past about the validity of our work as artists, we often run to say that it is culture, as if to say, "Oh, you wouldn't understand—it's a cultural thing." But if we say that we are sharing culture, then we are seen more as anthropologists than as serious artists (as Savigliano [2009] describes). This limits us because of the ways that value systems are configured in the academic institutions where we work. Under this system, anthropologists belong in another category. They are not "artists," and they deal only with excavating the "exotic" and "foreign." At times, we feel safer calling ourselves artists than culture bearers due to the sense that something that is "just art" is only about aesthetics, whereas culture carries with it all this baggage that must be carefully handled—and rightfully so. As culture bearers who teach in academic spaces, we run the risk of appropriating our own forms by dislocating them from their original contexts, creating the potential for cultural appropriation as we discussed in the previous chapter. The following interlude by Sinclair examines this idea of appropriation by a colonized body, looking at how oppositional aesthetic systems converge in his own dancing.

***

Interlude by Sinclair: Whose aesthetics belong to whom?

Some of the feedback I have gotten from outsiders on my dancing makes it clear that there is a disconnect between what people expect and what I actually bring to my performances. It is one thing to not like a performance, and of course one is entitled to their opinion. But it is another thing to dismiss it completely, as if to say, "What *was* that? Was that even a dance?" I remember a confrontation between myself and two of my colleagues—one a Ghanaian man, the other an African American woman—that took place when I was in graduate school. The latter approached me and my Ghanaian colleague, asking why we did not use our African dance practices to create positive disruptions in our university setting. She said that I used "contemporary dance" aesthetics in my work more than my own African dances, and she was concerned that neither of us seemed to dance like Africans. That is, we did not move in ways that Americans expect African dancers to move. As the conversation started to intensify, I deescalated it with just one question to her: "Have you ever taken my African dance class?" I had to make it clear to her that if she had taken one of my classes, she would have recognized that the "contemporary dance" she was referring to was actually from *Swange*, a Nigerian traditional dance deeply rooted in the Tiv culture. This dance is very different from other West African dance forms frequently performed in the United States. I can only describe this exchange between me and my American colleague as an aesthetic disconnect. She had particular expectations about what African dance should look like—and how an African man like me should move and create work—and was disappointed when I did not meet those expectations.

I am an African man practicing "contemporary dance" in the United States, where I fully embrace a wide variety of aesthetic values in my creative research and even in techniques while training myself and my students. Because of this mixing of aesthetic forms, I was once confronted by the accusation: "So, you talk about appropriation and how bad it can be for dance, but aren't you also appropriating Western contemporary dance?" referring to the contemporary, "pedestrian" movements that I incorporated into my work. I was, of course, thrown off by this assertion. This type of accusation is not usually directed at someone like me, a Black person. I dilly dallied for a minute or two and, in my head, I started to question my own authenticity, painfully reflecting on the fact that Nigeria had undergone a period of colonization, which is part of my cultural DNA. I speak in English, I write in English, and I went through very rigorous training throughout years of schooling to become a modern individual in a colonized world. Is my speaking English a sort of appropriation? My only option to practice "dance" as an "art form" in school, as opposed to dancing in my community, was to train in a studio, surrounded by books and videos about Western dance history.

As I thought about the accusation during this feedback session, I felt immense pain. As innocent as the question may have seemed, a type of trauma was inflicted on me that day—on my dance body, my history, and my artistic self. I felt discombobulated and disembodied at the same time. I tried to justify why this person would accuse me of this, and I was almost convinced that I was, in fact, appropriating Western culture. I went back to the popular argument that a Black person cannot be "racist," and thought for a second about how this can be true. I am not sure if, when a White person is confronted with this same accusation of cultural appropriation, they feel the same way that I did at that moment. Do they? But for me, the pain of knowing that I was forced by the world around me to become this type of modern artist in a globalized world was intensified when I realized that I cannot possibly be anything other than this. This is exactly what I feel every day teaching students about dance. I see their confusion and I see my limitations.

After I took a moment to think, I decided to say, with irritation, "No, I am not appropriating Western contemporary dance." While I was speaking those words, they felt new to my mouth. It felt like I had said something inversely and I felt, for a second, that I defended myself, my history, and my culture. When I draw on Western contemporary dance aesthetics, I am not appropriating. I am responding to the systemic expectations that I face in the dance field today, as a colonized person with little chance of regaining his authentic self since relocating to a new cultural space. So, I own what I have and express myself through that which I understand to be my own, which arises from a confluence of aesthetic expressions that may seem contradictory to some. I recognize that my voice as an artist is that of a conquered individual, but it is through this voice that I can fight to make space for myself and others like me.

***

The commodification of aesthetic values in dance

Judgments about what is "good" or "bad" in dance are often used to connect dancers to resources. Resources may be monetary but also include other forms of institutional support, like time, practice or performance space, and press coverage. There is a sense that investing in "bad" dance is a waste of money because it does not fit mainstream ideas about what dance or art is supposed to be. However, when we think about art, we should not be thinking about whether a form wastes resources, but instead about its underlying value and importance to the human experience. Are people having fun, expressing something, connecting with their community, feeling more relaxed or joyful, or achieving a spiritual state through a dance form? We know that when it comes down to dividing up resources to support some dances and not others, decisions must be made about what is worth supporting. Although resources may be limited, can we at least rethink the language of aesthetic judgment that we use to assign value in dance?

We are aware that there is resistance among some dancers, especially those working within traditional or community-based forms, to placing monetary value on dance because of the belief that dance should transcend money and economics. The idea of commodifying art and culture is offensive to some traditional artists because many believe that culture should not be sold as a product. We agree with this to an extent, but we also acknowledge that we live in a capitalist society where everything is monetized. We know that it is difficult for many professional dancers, regardless of what form they practice, to make a living wage. We are concerned with the reasons why some dancers feel forced or compelled to pursue their art as a hobby or a "passion project," or why dancers who come from traditional or folk cultures are so often accused of or insecure about selling out, being inauthentic, or breaking the rules of "tradition" if they decide to pursue their art professionally.

Some traditional or folk dancers want to participate as professionals in the dance market, but there is pressure to adapt the form to be more modern or spectacular to please audiences outside of their immediate community. This adaptation makes the dance more accessible in some ways, but the result is often spectacle-based and virtuosic, or "Westernized." For example, dances may take on aesthetic features from classical ballet, such as more verticality, turned-out feet, and extreme leg extensions. This is not to say that spectacle, virtuosity, and ballet technique are bad. But they make up just one way to dance. The professionalization and spectacularization of a community-based or folk form change a dance aesthetic in material ways, and the aesthetic shifts that arise from this process can have both positive and negative economic consequences for practitioners.

To take Irish dance as one example, the Riverdance phenomenon demonstrates the process of a folk or traditional form that has become fully globalized. This spectacle, which premiered as an intermission act at the 1994 Eurovision Song Contest, completely changed the ways that traditional Irish dance—and Ireland itself—were seen on the global stage. The costumes became sleeker and sexier, the steps became more virtuosic, and the rhythms were mixed with flamenco, tap, and Eastern European and Russian folk forms. In this "multicultural" spectacle, public perception of Irish dance changed dramatically. Some purists would say that it became too globalized, losing its unique Irishness and trading in its idyllic "dancing at the crossroads" aesthetic for a highly produced theatrical production. However, it also offered significant opportunities for professionalization in Irish dance. The proliferation and popularity of Irish dance profoundly changed the landscape of Irish dance training and career opportunities. Rather than competing until the age of about 18 and then quitting or opening up one's own school, Irish dancers could dream about touring the world as a cast member of one of the new Irish dance shows. As the Riverdance phenomenon (which included not just Riverdance, but a slew of other shows in the same vein) went global, many dancers retired from the shows and opened up schools throughout mainland Europe, Russia, Japan, and other countries that previously did not have large Irish dance communities.

Another unexpected outcome of Irish dance's spectacularization was that, as Catherine Foley notes, this global interest also translated to more interest in Irish dance at the local level (2001). This meant that mainstream competitive dance exploded, and previously underrepresented forms, like *sean-nós* from Connemara in the west of Ireland and other "old style" step dance forms from throughout Munster province, also became more popular as dancers sought to learn more about the history and aesthetic of other Irish dance styles. It seems counterintuitive, but the globalization of Irish dance opened up many opportunities for practitioners to explore the breadth of styles that exist, giving local communities a boost in resources and attention as well.

The commodification of dance cultures plays a large role in how we experience, interact with, and judge various forms of dance. In addition, in our digital world, dancers today are products of online corporatization and can sell their dancing skills globally on the web for views and likes. We must ask ourselves how we can utilize the power of this global exposure to sustain our own communities, finding new ways to exist and coexist within corporatized systems. This idea of coexistence is key. We recognize that dancers from all genres are fighting for limited resources, and it is hard to survive as a professional dancer and fight for equity, access, and inclusion as we all navigate a commodified world. Part of what we are confronting in this book is how such commodification has drastically altered the aesthetic systems by which our work is judged in various spaces, whether on stage, in the classroom, or on social media. We address issues of space in connection with performance aesthetics in greater detail in the following chapter. The following interlude by Kate reflects her experiences with exploring different aesthetic systems within Irish dance, and how exploring confluences with other forms, like Brazilian and African diasporic dances, within her body might promote kinesthetic empathy across these cultural systems.

***

Interlude by Kate: Building kinesthetic empathy through aesthetic exploration

I was one of the young Irish dancers whose horizons expanded with the dawn of Riverdance in the mid-1990s. I saw myself on stage someday, and I also became hungrier to take advantage of increased opportunities to delve deeper into the form. When I was in college and still competing, I went to a summer program at the University of Limerick in Ireland, where my ideas about Irish dance aesthetics were disrupted. There I learned about *sean nós* from Connemara for the first time. The style is "close to the floor," as they say. The shuffling footwork is low and "neat and tidy" under the body, in contrast to the high stepping, loud stomping, and jumping and leaping of mainstream competitive Irish dance. It is also improvisational. I remember learning the steps and thinking that they seemed pretty simple compared to the more "difficult" steps I had been competing with. I recall thinking that I could make them look even better by doing them with turned-out feet, crossed legs, higher kicks, and a little more vertical energy, effectively placing my competitive dance technique on top of them.

What I didn't realize at the time, of course, was that I completely missed the point of what is difficult about *sean nós* dancing—or, better said, I was not empathetic to what is valued in this form. As I learned more about *sean nós* in the coming years, I had to push away all those trained habits from competitive dance and replace them with a whole new technique. I had to sit into my hips more; I had to dance down more than up; I had to learn to make crisp sounds with my feet in parallel, rather than in a turned-out and over-crossed position. My heels and toes just didn't strike the floor the same way in the base position I had trained in.[3] And finally, what has taken even longer has been learning how to improvise within the style. This involves not just imitating and regurgitating steps that my teacher taught me, but actually listening to the music, dialoguing with the musician in real-time (if I'm lucky enough to be with one), and responding appropriately from moment to moment. I have had to learn how to build an improvisational toolkit based on building blocks from the *sean nós* vocabulary for each rhythm—whether reel, jig, or hornpipe. The idea of building an improvisational toolkit may seem basic to dancers in other percussive styles, but as a competitive Irish dancer, it was a revelation to me.

Today I cringe when I recall telling my *sean nós* teacher that the steps seemed "dirty," which I meant as physically more grounded and closer to the floor or earth ("dirt-y"). But this particular word carries a judgment with it and was triggering to my teacher. She looked offended when I said it, and I immediately knew I had said something wrong, but at the time I wasn't sure what. I still think about this moment often because I know that although I meant it innocently at the time, the words struck a nerve in her. My unintentional misstep came, perhaps, after years of being told (either explicitly or implicitly) that her dance form was less technical or respectable than competitive step dance, which receives so much more attention and is a booming international business, especially since Riverdance changed the landscape for Irish dance. Having just learned that another type of Irish dancing even existed, it went completely over my head that there would be any judgment associated with my comment, and it took me a few years of further training, research, and study to understand why my comment offended her.

As I delved more into different styles, I learned that the rigid competitive style is not the only way to engage with Irish dance. There is actually much more room for improvisation, playfulness, and adaptability, elements that I believe were buried under the image of what Irish nationalists in the early twentieth century wanted Irish dancing to be. Irish dancing has been promoted as an anti-colonial nationalist product for over a century, and Riverdance further promoted its global commodification. It makes me wonder: has Irish dance as a communally practiced form always been so rigid, or is what we usually see today the result of Ireland's colonial and postcolonial assertion of national identity?

Interestingly, learning about other ways to be an Irish dancer also led to my engagement with Brazilian and African diasporic forms, which opened the door for me to recognize and explore another side of traditional Irish dance that I thought had only one mode of aesthetic expression. Engaging with these new forms *did something* to me on a physical and psychological level. Competitive Irish dance is a Western(ized) form that ticks many of the boxes of what would be considered a Western European aesthetic with its extreme verticality, extension, and virtuosity. But I began to wonder if Irish dance was always this way, or if it had to be. My thinking around Irish dance—and my aesthetic relationship to it—changed after I started to learn these lesser-known Irish dance styles, along with Brazilian capoeira and West African dance at the same time. Before that, I was caught up in the "perfectionism" of Irish dance, which carried over into every aspect of my life. It was an aesthetic system that ruled me—I was obsessively disciplined, rigid, and could not adapt to change. When I took that first capoeira class, I felt a sense of freedom, which initially was just a physical feeling. Imagine an Irish dancer, stiff as a board, moving her torso, spine, arms, and head, and going upside down. Over time, I also started to notice the incorporation of Afro-Brazilian aesthetics and philosophies into my body. I began to interact with people and everyday situations with more flexibility and confidence. Experiencing and training different aesthetic streams within my body taught me the power we have to develop different ways of being in the world and to deepen our capabilities for kinesthetic empathy within confluent spaces.

***

Locating aesthetic values in dance

In dance, aesthetics develop through physical practice, and so we now turn to an examination of how aesthetics and technique are trained in dance cultures. We know that dancers define artistry in different ways, and it is not our goal in this chapter to offer a single definition. However, we do want to ask questions that prompt us to reflect further on how artists work and exist in various aesthetic contexts. In traditional or folk forms like the ones both of us practice, conversations often turn to defining the essence of a dance to distinguish it from other forms. This allows practitioners to describe an aesthetic system that authoritatively defines what is "good" or "bad" in technique, what is "authentic," and what comprises "artistry" in the form. We feel that we are constantly walking the line of saying, on one extreme, that "all dance is good, all people should dance;" and, on the other extreme, saying that to be a "good" and "authentic" dancer, one must be a trained virtuoso who comes from a long lineage of tradition and community. On a personal level, both of us want to define where we belong so that we can specify our worth. But we also want to do away with the definitions and categories that make us feel boxed in, even though, ironically, these are the only tools we currently have at our disposal to assess this worth. We believe that this demarcation is the result of Westernization, in which confluent spaces become divided by labels, brands, and cultural markers, rather than left open for the free flow of cross-cultural influences and sharing of ideas. As so-called "traditional" dancers, we want to think about how we give proper acknowledgment to our communities while also meeting our own desires to branch out, try new things, and collaborate with dancers from other forms.

When Sinclair first arrived in the United States from Nigeria, he found the training in modern dance that he was required to take as part of his M.F.A. program to be emotionally challenging. He felt that his own body knowledge was not valued by some of his teachers. The training violated his pride and sense of self. Students like Sinclair who come from other dance cultures and are forced to train in mainstream forms in order to progress through an academic program are at a disadvantage because they start at zero. They have to prove themselves in a new form, whereas those who are already trained in those forms are often not required to study any other dance cultures to complete their degrees. The experience can be demoralizing and humiliating, and the student may rarely, if ever, have an opportunity to show what they do well in the classroom. Sinclair had undergone intense dance training in Nigeria, so it was not that he was not ready for the physical demands. Rather, he found that his training in the United States was not only aimed at learning a new form but also actively countered the knowledge he already had. He felt as though his years of training in Nigeria were worthless. He also noted that the training was quite harsh and that enduring it seemed to be a rite of passage that was perpetuated as dancers went on to train their own students. Competitive success was emphasized as the most important component of dance. Such competition discourages the potential for collaboration among students, and especially the potential for organic collaboration among dancers from different dance cultures and training backgrounds.

Sinclair can describe clear differences between his modern dance classes in an American university and the traditional dance classes he took at his university in Nigeria. A modern class is often structured like a ballet class: students dance in the center of the studio ("center work"), go through a series of stretching exercises, engage in core strengthening ("core work"), and then dance across the studio in different spatial patterns ("across the floor"). Finally, the instructor leads students in more artistic movement generation and execution ("choreography"), followed by a "cool down," which might also include a discussion about discoveries made during class. Aesthetic values trained in such classes often include release, flow, and precision, with a focus on creative individual expression.

In contrast, college-level dance classes in Nigeria are usually geared toward the cooperative practice of traditional dances with the goal of preserving embodied community knowledge. Teaching is centered around the articulation of body parts in a broad array of aesthetic choices, movement vocabularies, and vocal articulations of multi-tonal and phonetic proficiencies through singing. Teachers focus on equipping students with the tools of storytelling, dramatization, reflection, as well as a patriotic awareness of the nation's history and kingdoms. Exercises are geared toward strengthening the legs, endurance, and general fitness. The class is accompanied by drums and rhythms that guide the body through traditional movements.

One notable element of college-level Nigerian dance classes is the practice of having students choose from a variety of traditional dances to practice during each session. The chosen dances are selected through a democratic voting process. After the class chooses a particular dance, students act out specific roles that correspond to the roles within the selected dance community, including instrumental accompanists, singers, and dancers. All aspects of the traditional dance event are performed with the goal of passing on cultural knowledge and building strong cohesion. For example, if a class chooses to learn and perform the royal *Ugho* dance of the Benin people, women play roles such as royal wives, queen mothers, and noble society women, and men are divided into subsections of chiefs, kingsmen, and high society men. Other subgroups include maidens, hands men, palace servants and helpers, orators, musicians, and calisthenic sword dancers. Students also learn to make costumes, play instruments, and handle weapons and other props. By acting out all the dramatics of the tradition, they understand that they are not just performers, but also culture bearers. They learn to dance with the people and things that circulate within that cultural context. They learn the behavioral "scripts" that are associated with each element. A "good" dancer can play all or most roles (including across genders) and can sing as the traditional peoples would. The practice is less about the perfection of the individual body as a surface for aesthetic judgment and evaluation. Instead, meaning is found in the collective doing.

One of the challenges that Sinclair encounters when teaching African dance forms in American colleges is that, unlike the *Ugho* dance of the Benin people described above, many of the non-mainstream Nigerian dances that he teaches have very little or no codified training or techniques, nor do they have systems that distinguish "good" from "bad" dance. Because academia requires student evaluation, Sinclair struggles to codify what "good" dancing is in the forms he teaches in order to judge the skills of his students and evaluate their progress. In addition, Sinclair has found in conversations with some of his African dance colleagues that they believe they are not qualified to teach dance because of this inability to evaluate training and progress. To be a "good dancer" in a Western context can also mean adopting a more virtuosic style, as described earlier. Virtuosity is often easier to evaluate on stage and in the classroom because it aligns with specific standards defined within a form, but this approach misses a lot of the cultural substance that promotes kinesthetic empathy, which deals with the "spaces between" movers in social situations to build interpersonal trust and understanding (Reynolds and Reason 2012).

The process of honing a technique to become a "good dancer" often begins with imitation, as we explained in the previous chapter, but we have noticed that classically trained students often come in with an attitude of "show me and I will show you I can do it" that is antithetical to the approach that communal dance cultures espouse. In a community context, people pick up movements by watching, imitating, and reciprocating each other's energy. There is also a sense among highly trained dancers in any form that they will be able to easily pick up a new one, even if it comes from an entirely different set of aesthetic and cultural values, like Kate thinking, as a competitive step dancer, that she could easily pick up and improve the *sean nós* steps she learned. In the context of a professionally equipped dance studio with mirrors, many classically trained students learning the techniques of other dance cultures become concerned with the "doing" of the steps and obsess over doing them perfectly. Teachers simply cannot recreate the original setting and all the elements of the dance culture in its fullest expression. We ask ourselves: How do we get around these limitations? Do we not belong in these spaces? Does it do everyone a disservice—both the communities we come from and our students—to offer this kind of class in higher education if we cannot convey a dance culture's full context and meaning? How do we teach what value in dance feels like in the body?

***

Interlude by Sinclair: The feeling of aesthetic value

In December of 2005, I was in my second year of college. The first semester had just ended, and everyone had gone home for the holidays. My mentor, Dr. Chris Ugolo, invited me and another student to attend a dance concert. I had never seen traditional dance performed on a proscenium stage before that evening. A group of about a dozen men stormed the stage, each holding small metal gongs. They ran onto the stage in a single file, playing fast, melodious tempos on the gongs as they made a circle formation. This dance lasted about ten minutes and I was transfixed throughout. I did not move and hardly blinked. I was stupefied. My jaw dropped. I was drawn to the circular formation, the use of the gong as the only instrument, and the stomping of feet—the jumping, running, and vibrating with complex footwork. After the last run and jump that brought the men to their knees, punctuated by a blackout on stage, my heart was racing! On my feet clapping, I looked over at my mentor and he nodded his head with a knowing smile. As we sat down for the closing, he said to me, "Have you ever seen anything like that?" I said to him, "No, but I didn't want it to end. And I want to dance for the rest of my life."

That day did change my life. A few years later, between 2009 and 2012, I would dance with that state dance troupe and even choreograph for them. That performance was not the first time I had seen traditional dance, of course, but it was the first time I had seen it in a proscenium setting. Why did I react this way? Did the elevation that the proscenium stage provided elevate my senses about my own traditional dances? I felt affirmed to also see my dances up there and it was a defining moment for understanding my aesthetic preferences in dance. As a minority in a world replete with voices and dances from dominant groups, I started to appreciate the visibility gained any time my forms are displayed on a bigger stage.

For me, aesthetics in dance is what draws you in. It is a feeling that we, as a field, have not yet been able to come up with the right terminology to describe. I remember the excitement I felt as a student when I heard drums playing and how I would run to the studio the moment I heard them. Sound is a big part of this feeling. But I believe that aesthetic value is an all-encompassing feeling, maybe one that involves freedom that allows you to see yourself in a performance without any or few conflicting feelings about negative judgments. For me, it is being in a space to dance and feeling free to be myself, accompanied by the feeling that I am allowed to dream and decide how I dance and how I interact with those I am dancing with. Another factor could be language—hearing people speak my language and receiving praise encourages me to dance more. I know exactly how the community feels about my dancing. I love to dance and I appreciate it when the community affirms my presence in the space and values who I am. Getting anything less than this type of feeling or seeing people not understand my aesthetic choices results in disappointment for both me as the performer and them as the audience. This, I have found, is what really makes people judge a dance form as simply "good" or "bad." I think it is ultimately about expectations that fit into one's preconceived notions about what is aesthetically pleasing.

I believe it is possible to expand expectations to capture more than one set of aesthetic values. For example, in 2008, I started my own dance company in Nigeria. I recruited six men and four women to join my company. To start with something more comfortable, I first taught some movements from familiar Nigerian dance vocabularies. Later, I began to incorporate some Western styles as well. Introducing Western dance to Nigerian dancers was very taxing because they overtly valued their Nigerian aesthetics over the Western contemporary ideas that I brought into the studio. But after months of training, the dancers began to love using Western aesthetics to express themselves. One day, one of the dancers said, "You don't know what you have done for me and all of us." Out of curiosity, I asked, "But what did I do?" He responded by describing how much he appreciated my willingness to go through such a tedious process to help them see the need to diversify their dancing. They had seen tremendous growth in the way their bodies had taken on new shapes and emotional expressions. He found a new clarity in his ideas about movement. He felt that, although he came from a long line of dancers and entertainers, he had gained a certain type of maturity through the learning process—a process that made him more aware of his own dance culture, as well as the tools that he could garner from other aesthetic systems.

I tell this story to point out that I am not against Western aesthetics—I see their value. My point is that we all benefit from diversifying our aesthetic training and repertoire. We may not adopt every element into our practice, but I believe art is meant to be shared, experienced, and shaped by us as artists. We can use other aesthetic values and systems to help sustain our own. In this way, different aesthetic vernaculars allow for positive contributions rather than breed negative competition. There is room for more than one aesthetic. The body is a malleable surface and there is so much good that can come from the willingness to include others while wholeheartedly giving students our knowledge so that they can grow within their own practice. I will be the first to admit that I was one of those who used my own ideas about what "perfect" aesthetics in dance are to dismiss those dance forms that did not meet what I knew to be dance and, in fact, "good dance." I had to attend national events in Nigeria to see, interact with, and witness others dance their best, and I had to learn how much they individually value their own forms before I could start to see the value of forms that were different from mine. It became a goal of mine to experience as many dance cultures as possible in order to become someone that can respect, value, and engage with others, even if I don't fully understand them. I cannot say that I completely enjoy all dances, but I have come to appreciate many more since being exposed to new aesthetic systems through my experiences in confluent spaces.

***

Conclusion

Aesthetic systems are built over time and depend on the space the dance is practiced in, the people who practice it, and their reasons for participating. In this chapter, we have asked whether individuals who do not see themselves as "artists" in the Western sense can also see themselves as producers of art and as producers of culture, simultaneously. We want to recognize how individual and collective bodies also have intellects of their own, and how the embodied knowledge that we carry helps us develop kinesthetic empathy across cultural systems. We believe it is important for those who do not necessarily see themselves as culture bearers to consider how all dance puts the body in a position to behave in culturally specific ways. In the following chapter, we consider how space shapes the ways that we navigate aesthetic expectations and transpose cultural values in migratory, confluent settings.

Notes

1 We can also describe such a collective as "communitas," as described by anthropologist Victor Turner (1986).
2 This interlude is excerpted and adapted from Kate's essay, "O Corpo é Tudo," written for *Incomum Revista* (Spanos 2021).
3 Catherine E. Foley refers to the work of adapting to a new aesthetic as requiring a "multi-sensory method of transmission [that involves] proprioceptive training and somatic sensation" (2020, 312).

References

Bernstein, Robin. 2009. "Dances with Things: Material Culture and the Performance of Race." *Social Text* 101: 67–94.
ConVIDA! – Conversa Cabôca Com Joab Jó (PE). 2020. SescBrasil. https://www.youtube. com/watch?v=TCZcOsa0K10.
Davis, Crystal U. 2022. *Dance and Belonging: Implicit Bias and Inclusion in Dance Education*. Jefferson, NC: McFarland.
Foley, Catherine E. 2001. "Perceptions of Irish Step Dance: National, Global, and Local." *Dance Research Journal* 33: 34–45.
———. 2020. "Steps, Style and Sensing the Difference: Transmission and the Re-Contextualisation of Molyneaux's Traditional Set Dances within the Irish Traditional Dance Competitive Arena." *Research in Dance Education* 21 (3): 312–27. https://doi.org/ 10.1080/14647893.2020.1776242.

Gaztambide-Fernández, Rubén. 2020. "The Orders of Cultural Production." *Journal of Curriculum Theorizing* 35 (3): 5–27.

Gaztamide-Fernández, Rubén A., Amelia M. Kraehe, and B. Stephen Carpenter II. 2018. "The Arts as White Property: An Introduction to Race, Racism, and the Arts in Education." In *The Palgrave Handbook of Race and the Arts in Education*, edited by Amelia M. Kraehe, Rubén A. Gaztamide-Fernández, and B. Stephen Carpenter II, 1–31. Cham, Switzerland: Palgrave Macmillan.

Reynolds, Dee, and Matthew Reason. 2012. *Kinesthetic Empathy in Creative and Cultural Practices*. Bristol, UK: Intellect.

Savigliano, Marta. 2009. "Worlding Dance and Dancing Out There in the World." In *Worlding Dance*, edited by Susan Leigh Foster, 163–90. Basingstoke, NY: Palgrave Macmillan.

Souza, Jessé. 2018. *A classe média no espelho: sua história, seus sonhos e ilusões, sua realidade*. Rio de Janeiro: Estação Brasil.

Spanos, Kathleen A. 2021. "O Corpo é Tudo: Theory, Practice and Resistance in the Body." *Incomum Revista* 2 (1): 1–14.

Turner, Victor W. 1986. "Carnival in Rio: Dionysian Drama in an Industrializing Society." In *The Anthropology of Performance*, 103–24. New York, NY: PAJ Publications.

3 Navigating cultural confluences and envisioning new spaces

Interlude by Sinclair: Confluence Town

After graduating from high school, I was conflicted as to what I would study at university. On the one hand, I wanted to study something that was valuable to my parents, like medical sciences, accounting, law, or banking. But I secretly loved arts and literature. My teachers discouraged me from pursuing this path, and my first college advisor once told me that the arts were a "nuisance," referring to the theatre arts students dancing outside and making noise on their traditional drums. After two years of failing entrance exams at the University of Jos for law, account-ing, and English language courses, my mother took me to the university advisor to find any remedial courses (diploma, as it is called in Nigeria) for me to take while I awaited another round of law exam results. The advisor told us there was an opening in the theatre arts program. He said that he didn't think I could cope with being a theatre student, seeing how quiet, reserved, and subdued I seemed. But he also said there was no reason why I wouldn't get in since they were always look-ing to enroll more students. I signed up for the remedial course, and when we got home, my brother and I went out to get the examination form for me to apply to a four-year theatre arts degree program at the University of Benin, a highly ranked university in Nigeria.

While waiting for my results, I was a student in the theatre arts diploma program at the University of Jos for three months. It started off very rough. All the Shake-speare I read couldn't save me from feeling like a complete failure who couldn't act, sing, or dance. I was just too shy. Worst of all, when I got back home among my family and friends, I avoided any questions regarding what I was studying at school because I didn't want to be seen as a disappointment. Finally, my results from the University of Benin entrance exam came out. I passed the arts exam with flying colors and my mother couldn't stop talking about it, even though she avoided tell-ing people that I got in to study theatre. I withdrew from the diploma program at the University of Jos, where I had grown a lot and even played a lead character in the play *Banner of Peace* by Best Ugala and danced in the world premiere of Professor Irene Isoken Salami's *Much More Than Dancing*.

I packed my bags and headed to the University of Benin, never to return to Jos, Plateau State. As we headed south, we approached Lokoja, known as

DOI: 10.4324/9781003231226-4

"The Confluence Town" in Kogi State, a place where motorists and travelers stop to take a break, eat, and freshen up before heading back out on their long journeys. Confluence Town is a well-known Nigerian landmark with enough stories to last hundreds of lifetimes. As we got closer to the city, strangers who had been very quiet throughout the bus ride suddenly started chatting about Lokoja's colonial history and Lord Frederick Lugard, the governor of the then-Northern Protectorate and the Colony and Protectorate of Southern Nigeria, who ended slavery and amalgamated and named Nigeria (his mistress actually did the naming). According to the stories, Lokoja was his favorite town because of its unique river confluence at the center of Nigeria where the rivers Benue (from the east) and Niger (from the west) meet. As the storytellers got louder, the smell of food, smoke, cooked fish and meat, and fried plantains filled the bus. I smiled as I remembered how my mother would always say, "Chatters get louder when it is close to dinner time." As the bus came to a stop, I got off with everyone else to stretch, yawn, and wipe sweat from my forehead while dusting the harmattan sands off my body. It was time to eat.

Nigeria is known for its ethnic differences, religious conflicts, and political discords. It is a country where a small skirmish can instantly divide a group of people into warring enemies in the span of a few minutes. Even though we Nigerians know this to be true, we never fail to add that Nigeria is also a great country, made up of many different cultures. We have majority groups like the Igbo, Hausa, and Yorubas, while others like the Urhobos (my group), Gwarris, Nupes, Igalas, Tivs, and many others are referred to as minorities and are lesser known to outsiders. As I got off the bus in Confluence Town, I took note of how much we travelers had in common, despite coming from so many different places. The need for food and rest, and the excitement of meeting new people while traveling to a new place or heading back to a familiar one made us seem not so different after all. People greeted each other and asked, "Where are you going?" with pleasantries and laughter. Some even volunteered to show others where to get good Ogbono and Egusi soups and other delicacies. Lokoja calmed my nerves during this very intense and anxiety-filled trip to Benin City as I transitioned from one stage of my life to the next.

Back on the bus, set for Benin, memories of my time at the University of Jos flooded my mind. I thought about all the trees on campus that I used to sit under, where I would work on my lines and monologues and pull my thoughts together. I hoped to find a similarly quiet space in Benin City. As my bus pulled up to the Ekehuan campus of the University of Benin, I looked to the right and immediately noticed a group of mature trees next to some tennis courts. These trees would become my place of solace. Over the next few months, I came to see this place as a meeting point like Lokoja, where I could work through my internal struggles in a space of tranquility. It became my own personal Confluence Town, a place so safe that I was able to think through creative ways to survive the challenges of being a student and artist in Nigeria. I needed an escape from spaces like the campus assembly hall, which was a place strictly for rehearsing and performing on the proscenium stage. Occasional bystanders and unwanted visitors used to pass through the hall and peer into rehearsals, and I would feel judged on my delivery of lines and movement patterns, restricted from fully expressing myself. I also felt the tensions between Western vs. non-Western artistic and educational systems; my family's expectations vs. my artistic inclinations; English as my colonial language vs. my local tongues; and contemporary vs. traditional Nigerian dance practices. So I built a routine around sitting under the trees where I could rest my body, reflect on my potential, and allow myself to flow in and out of the different cultural identities, practices, and ideas that were converging within me.

Today I still feel these tensions within myself as a dancer who has migrated between different spaces throughout my life. Sometimes I feel like I don't belong anywhere or that I have to fit into the molds that cultural stereotypes about a person like me dictate. I feel that I sit at the intersection of my colonial and postcolonial identities that arise from growing up in Nigeria and working as a dancer in the United States. I like Chinua Achebe's description of himself in early postcolonial Nigeria in the 1960s as being at the intersection of colonial and postcolonial ambivalence (2009). I feel the remnants of this historical ambivalence, even though I am generations apart from him. In school, I was taught about my Nigerian culture through Western colonial training, which means that I understand myself through cultural stereotypes. My formal dance training happened in college, in Western-style studios. And because I now inhabit this ambivalent space while living in the United States, I must rely on these stereotypes about where I come from to explain and justify who I am.

Now that I am in the United States, I feel that I am neither Nigerian nor American. I am country-less. The only things I can hold onto are my learned attitudes, dances, and memories of the homes I have inhabited throughout my life. As someone who has always used the notion of "land" or geographical location as a way to center and identify myself, not having one place I can call my own makes me feel that I am "nowhere." I have to develop a strong sense of self within my own body that is not reliant on a particular place, and dance helps me do that. I am an African dancer who has been empowered by the very voices and ideologies that I dare to fight against. Dance is the only tool that I have to navigate the confluences that I find myself in.

***

Confluent spaces and fields in motion

Throughout this book, we theorize confluences as the ever-shifting spaces where streams of cultural expression meet, interact with, and influence each other. We have set the stage for developing this framework by examining the dynamics of language and aesthetic value in confluent spaces. In this chapter, we delve more deeply into what we mean by confluence in dance by examining the structure of spaces in which dances take place, considering how those spaces shape our practices and experiences as dancers. We examine the spaces in which our bodies move and interact with other bodies, and how conventional Western spaces for dance training and performance shape expectations about what dance should be and how we should behave as performers, spectators, participants, and community members.

Expanding ideas about how space is used in dance requires that we recognize that many dance cultures grow and flourish outside of studios and off stages—in streets, homes and kitchens, community centers, and nightclubs. We consider how tacit assumptions about a dancer or dance culture reinforce the notion that everyone can thrive in Western-designed spaces and that those spaces are the ideal venues for creative success.

Thinking about architecture as a tangible representation of the human desire to carve out one's own space and territory, we consider how such structures can be designed in ways that make some people feel welcome while others feel excluded. We believe that conversations about diversity and inclusion in the dance field often do not address the spaces we are expected to dance in and how these spaces do not allow practitioners of all dance cultures to thrive. Simply inviting more dancers from non-mainstream dance cultures into spaces that have not been designed for them to succeed is not enough. Reconsiderations of how we create and use space will, we believe, lead to more inclusive and equitable representation in our field.

To examine where confluences in dance take place, we conceptualize space in the following ways: (1) as a geographical location; (2) as an architectural structure or spatial design; (3) as a physical surface upon which to dance; and (4) as the dancing body itself, a space within which confluent streams converge. Conversations about space often focus on the details of physical structure and architecture, suggesting that these structures provide culturally coded cues about how to behave and interact. Reciprocally, we also consider how the cultural codes embedded in a dancer's body shape how they inhabit the space. That is, how we take up space is determined by our culturally learned behaviors, as well as the cultural migrations that we experience as moving bodies dancing in the world. Examining migrations prompts us to consider the spaces that dance practices originate from or relocate to—and the people who carry these practices with them as they migrate—to understand how confluent streams shift as we move and change.

The opening interlude by Sinclair about passing through Lokoja, the Confluence Town, during his journey from Jos to Benin City reflects the ways that we think about confluence as both a physical site where social interactions take place and as the dancing body within which cultural influences and experiences converge. The coming together of many different people in Confluence Town was mirrored in his experience of sitting under the trees at the University of Benin, where he felt the convergence of cultural influences and ideologies from his past and present. Space is not only the physical structure in which we dance, move, and interact with other people. It also represents how our bodies are spaces that accumulate cultural capital and gain and transmit cultural knowledge.

As noted in previous chapters (Introduction and Chapter 1), our framework of confluent spaces expands on the notion of contact zones, which Oxford Reference defines as "social places (understood geographically) and spaces (understood ethnographically) where disparate cultures meet and try to come to terms with each other." They are "often trading posts or border cities, cities where the movement of peoples and commodities brings about contact" ("Contact Zone," n.d.). We see confluence in dance as not only the sites where people and cultures meet (contact zones), but also as the dancing body that amasses and performs those cultural encounters. The body is always located in a particular place and dancers sense how they exist in that place. According to ethnomusicologists Steven Feld and Keith H. Basso, we derive a "sense of place" as we "encounter places, perceive them, and invest them with significance" (1996, 4). Encountering a place as a culturally defined space means experiencing its history and the people involved in that history (Solomon 2000). In music, Feld refers to the potentiality of place as an "acoustemology of flow," which describes how the "sonic presence and awareness of music shapes how people make sense of experiences," linking together fluid paths and creating embodied memories (1996, 97). For dancers, a sense of place is tangible as their physical bodies move through space. Through culturally defined movement, dancers imbue a physical place with significance to create a destination, thought, emotion, or memory. Central to our framework, then, is this interaction between the body as a site of confluence within physical spaces that also, in turn, have confluent bodies moving through them. We highlight the experience of the migratory dancing body, transected by many cultural cross-streams and interacting with other such bodies in shared spaces.

In dance, a principal site for consideration is the stage or studio, which are spaces where mainstream Western forms are typically performed. In academia, the stage or studio is sometimes pitted against more communal spaces, such as parties, parades, processions, clubs, or ritual spaces. Both of us dance on stage and in performance settings, as well as in communal contexts. Even as we see the delineation between these spaces, each space is still equally part of our experiences as we continuously travel in and out of them. Highlighting the dynamic and shifting nature of transcultural spaces, the essayists in *Fields in Motion: Ethnography in the Worlds of Dance* (Davida 2011) examine how transnational and "multi-hyphenated" artists from dance cultures around the world navigate the realm of concert dance. The authors anthropologically examine dance in the "art world" to illustrate how dancers, as cultural knowledge bearers, experience "fields in motion" that overlap and cross paths while they create for the concert stage. In this chapter, we expand on this work by examining the migratory experience of dancers moving between the stage and more communal, less presentational spaces, considering how cultural forms can be transposed between these spatial configurations. In confluent dance spaces, "fields in motion" do not just overlap and cross, but they also envelop other cultural ideas and practices or become enveloped themselves, as the boundaries between mainstream and non-mainstream expand, contract, and shift.

We are particularly concerned with bodies that find themselves in migratory transitions and how the design of external structures defines their experience. Migration from one place to another often means that we dance in new spatial configurations that constrain us in different ways but can also open up new opportunities for innovation and discovery. Diasporic migration, in particular, involves a sense of "home" and "away from home" that is not only influenced by the physical structures in which people dance but also by the cultural surroundings in which they move. Our framework for cultural confluences in dance considers how the migratory body translates culturally specific language, transposes aesthetic values, and engages in learning, sharing, and negotiating with the organizational systems that provide a physical and cultural structure for dancers to practice in. The final section of this chapter examines a collaborative work that we, as migratory artists, created in an effort to translate our own cultural values from non-mainstream forms into a Western performance space.

This chapter also introduces the use of dialogue in this book to share our conversations on a more intimate level. We are two dancers whose cultural origins and journeys are very different, but we share the experience of becoming aware of the confluences in our bodies as we have moved through various spaces. Presenting our ideas about space in dialogue form points to how our interactions as co-authors and collaborators have been shaped by confluences. This format demonstrates how our framework can account for the migrations and cultural translations and transpositions that we experience in dance.

***

Dialogue: Taking up space in the classroom

Sinclair: When I was on the faculty job hunt, one of the colleges I interviewed at was a model school for North American dance programs. The studios were many and large. They had a floating studio and amazing ultramodern equipment and the staff to match. To me, coming from the outside, the meticulous design reflected the height of Western education and civilization. It was clear from the space itself that people would pay hefty sums to attend such a program. The students I taught in my hour-and-a-half modern dance class showed incredible skill—what I call "body facilities"—and most of them had already found ways to bring their ballet fundamentals into whatever form they were presented with. I suspected that most of those students must have been dancing in such an environment for a very long time. I confirmed this when I asked some of them when they started dancing, and they eagerly told me that they had been dancing as early as the age of three. They obviously felt comfortable in the space. I looked at the incredible facilities and the human infrastructure available at this institution—the technical skills that these students brought to the space. I could not keep myself from thinking about how lucky the professors were to have such an abundance of resources. These students were given the stage to succeed. They could walk into a college dance program with ease and feel welcome and at home in the space that had been provided for them. They already fit right into the performance aesthetic and culture that the faculty expected of them.

Kate: I know what you mean. There is an expectation in many college dance programs that students have classical dance training. I spoke to a student one time, a hip-hop dancer who wanted to become a professional dancer. She told me that she was taking ballet because it is "the foundation of all dance." I spoke to another student who had grown up dancing Bharatanatyam and she was taking a full load of ballet, modern, and hip-hop in order to "catch up" to her classmates. I have felt these same pressures to fit in. There is something about entering these spaces and immediately feeling like we don't belong because our "body facilities," as you call them, don't seem to fit what the studio facilities call for. Even if a studio itself may be familiar, the etiquette and unspoken rules of the studio space dictate how dancers interact and judge each other. That's why it's interesting that you had the opportunity, as a teacher, to flip the script and guide how students interacted. How did they respond to your class?

Sinclair: The students I taught during that interview seemed suspicious of me and what I brought to the classroom. In a system where our efforts are quantified by the effective deliverables of a product, so-called "excellence," and financial impact, being in this space is hard for me. In academia, we produce dance pieces, and our work is evaluated at the same level as people who are already part of the system. When you place me and my African styles into academia, it is hard to produce works that can compete because my students have never seen my dances before and I cannot fully introduce them to the cultural context without taking them to my home in Nigeria. I have to bring Nigeria into the studio with my own singular body. I must then teach rudimentary ideas and explain—sometimes even defend—my culture every time I teach. Also, because the students and individuals we cast for our choreographic works already feel at home in these spaces, they come in with a sense of privilege and the assumption that they already understand what we are trying to do. These assumptions come up, for instance, when I am teaching them African contemporary forms that require entirely different interactions with the space and with each other. This hinders learning, understanding, and appreciation of what I, as the teacher, bring to the creative process.

Kate: We are bringing non-mainstream forms into the space, but our students may not realize that doing so also requires a reconfiguration of how we use the space itself. Instead of dancing in rows in front of the mirror and imitating the instructor, we might ask them to engage with each other in a circle facing one another. This can be really disconcerting for some, and it may feel like they are being asked to break the rules. While some happily participate, others resist. The burden is on us as educators to both redefine the way they are going to use space—to convey that this is something different that they do not yet understand—and to also welcome them into that space.

Sinclair: It is a challenge, and sometimes I question why I am invited into these spaces at all. Although my skill set is essential for diversity, equity, and inclusion initiatives to succeed, the way these spaces are designed does not position me or my students to succeed in higher education. Although I can teach in these classrooms, like I did at that fancy school where I was interviewed, and as I do every day in my current position, the studio is simply not where my kind of dancing happens. The experiential aspect through which I teach and transmit my embodied knowledge is lost. For example, one element that the studio space is not designed for is the facilitation of music and sound for African dance. I have been told to be quiet or to close the door while teaching with live drumming. Without the musicians and modalities for high-note drumming and loud ululation, the essence of African dance is lost. Whatever is produced becomes a muffle of whitewashed African forms that can be hard to recognize for someone from my community. Although I am used to being in these spaces now, I still feel uncomfortable and displaced every time I enter the studio.

Kate: I relate to the issue of being too loud! Percussive dancers are always too loud, and we always have to be worried about ruining the floors, which I understand. We often end up dancing on marley, which is less than ideal for some percussive dancers, both in terms of the aesthetic sound that is produced and in terms of comfort and safety for our bodies. For example, tap dancers often complain that the stickiness of marley is bad for their joints because of the shoes they wear and how they use the floor. I don't think it would be hard to accommodate what we do but finding the funding and resources that would accommodate these forms is just not prioritized. If diversity and inclusion initiatives are supposed to invite more dancers from more dance cultures to be in these spaces, then why do we still have to conform to spatial configurations that hold us back from practicing our craft or might even physically injure us?

Sinclair: The struggles that we have experienced both as educators and students in these studios have arisen from expectations about who and what should be in these spaces, as well as how dancers from different cultural forms have been trained to behave in certain environments. We have to keep in mind how spaces convey aesthetic values and expectations, and dancers from non-mainstream forms experience tensions and confusion about where they belong. Diversity, equity, and inclusion initiatives claim to invite more non-mainstream dancers into mainstream spaces and provide them with equitable resources, but we must examine how those dancers thrive (or don't) in different environments and whether they need different resources. If not, the risk is further silencing and discouraging the very people who are being invited in. We have to create more flexibility in the ways that dancers are expected to use such spaces to express their cultural values.

***

The design of dance spaces

In the dance field in the United States, we have noticed a general belief that a dance studio or stage is the only canvas upon which to create artistic work. These spaces dictate what dances should be danced; how those dances should be learned and performed; what the body of the dancer should be able to do; how the instruction should be administered; how an accompanist or instrumentalist should behave; and who is allowed to share the space. Space dictates how bodies associate and interact with each other. A space determines how a body exists within it, from behavior and dress to expressions of aesthetic tastes, cultural values, and ideological beliefs. When we, as dancers, enter a space, we immediately perceive a sense of what type of dance product can and should come out of that space. Such structures for dance are not culturally neutral. They are designed with a particular "brand" in mind and further contribute to shaping that brand. Such physical spaces reinforce the meta-phorical "lanes" that we described in previous chapters that we, as dancers from non-mainstream forms, feel pressured to stay within.

Space is an important component of a dance class structure, and the design of that space shapes how dancers learn. Take the example of a "typical [Western] dance studio," which Susan Leigh Foster describes in this way: "A piano or a sound system may be located in one corner, a ballet barre might run along one or two walls, mirrors might line the other two walls, but the space contains no other defining features" (2019, 58). She explains how this spatial configuration "exerts a significant influence" on the dancing that takes place within the studio by placing dancers in rows facing the mirrors, contributing to the standardization and individualization of the practice. Studio components like marley floors, barres, mirrors, and a piano stand out as foreign to someone who has never danced in such a space and can become a deterrent or a distraction, intimidating them and stifling their creativity. A piano may suggest that a particular style of music should be played in that space. Marley may be inappropriate flooring for some dancers. And mirrors may force a kind of self-consciousness or presentational style that is antithetical to some community-focused dance forms. It is not that the two of us do not appreciate a beautiful dance studio and cannot work in one, but we can only practice certain elements of our dance cultures in these spaces. We know there is so much more to dance than what can take place within a studio. As dancers working in academia, the challenge is that we often only have the opportunity to show (and be evaluated on) a more presentational aspect of our work in these limited and limiting spaces.

When Kate went to Brazil to study frevo dance, a street carnival dance from the metropolitan region of Recife, she took lessons and participated in events with multiple groups in various spaces. Different frevo class structures exemplify how the dance is shaped by the space it is practiced in. Frevo is performed on stages during carnival and throughout the year, but its natural environment is in the streets, characterized by a massive agglomeration of people who dance behind and around frevo orchestras of brass and percussion instruments. (This configuration is different from the parade-like structure of Rio de Janeiro's famous samba carnival.) Groups offer frevo dance classes in various locations throughout the year—both indoors in dance studios with mirrors and outside in city squares. Studio classes tend to be more focused on visual presentation and virtuosic execution of moves, including high jumps in the air, deep squats to the ground, and big smiles, in a style that is referred to as "stage frevo." Students dance in rows facing the mirror with the teacher at the front. "Street frevo" classes, on the other hand, aim to recreate the experience of dancing during carnival, and the aesthetic of such classes promotes a more inclusive philosophy that says that anyone can dance frevo. Street frevo dancers often practice in a *roda* ("wheel," or circular formation) or change spatial configurations throughout the class. The style is more internally focused and interactive. Kate's street frevo teachers explained that dancing without a mirror or a "front" encourages students to take up the three-dimensional space around them, rather than constrain themselves to the two-dimensionality required to present toward an audience. For example, one step, called *tesoura* ("scissors"), is two-dimensional in stage frevo, with the shoulders, torso, and hips all in line, facing the front throughout the step, whereas street frevo dancers alternate between facing the front and either side, with the idea that others surround them and there is not just an audience in front of them. This orientation forces them to focus more on their own pleasure and that of those dancing with them, rather than on non-participatory spectators. Finally, two of the street frevo groups that Kate danced with always ended class with a *confusão* ("confusion"), which is a type of mosh pit experience that involves lots of elbowing, pushing, jumping into each other, and shouting. The *confusão* creates a joyous feeling of community that reflects Recife's carnivalesque spirit.[1]

In the context of Western theatres and performance venues, spatial designs are configured based on aesthetics, functionality, and cultural values that align with the Western mainstream. These designs may not serve all dancers, their dance traditions, and what they aim to achieve while dancing. While a proscenium performance in any form can create a stunning effect, the separation of performer and audience cuts off the opportunity for participation and interaction that is central to some dance cultures. One large hindrance in Western theatre spaces is the expectation that audiences adhere to etiquette and keep quiet during a performance. As Sinclair noted in the last chapter about what aesthetics feel like in his body, positive feedback from those around him is a crucial element of his dancing. Without that audible encouragement, the space feels empty and unsupportive. The issue of performer/audience separation in Western performance spaces is well known, and yet it is still common in academic dance spaces for the proscenium theatre to be the expected spatial configuration for performance and evaluation. We see proscenium performance as a great opportunity for social or communal dance forms to gain mainstream visibility, but we also see the limitations of presenting in such spaces. Sometimes audiences are encouraged to respond audibly or get up and dance from their seats, but the space creates a clear separation between performer and audience that hinders participation, or at the very least makes such participation awkward in a space that seems to demand silence and stillness. There is a sense of sanctity in these spaces that tells people to be quiet and "respectful," but we must understand that respect itself is culturally defined. In fact, in some cultures, it is disrespectful to not respond and actively participate. While we do not see a problem with the proscenium setup per se, we are concerned with the pervasive idea that performing on stage is the only way for a performer or a dance form to gain legitimacy.

In another example from Brazilian carnival traditions, Kate and her partner Pablo de Oliveira have been producing concerts by bands and artists from Brazil in the Washington, D.C., area together since 2015. One issue that frequently comes up is finding a venue that is flexible enough to allow people to participate in the performance in ways that are similar to how they would participate in Brazil. For example, one year they brought a street carnival band from Rio de Janeiro that would normally perform on top of a truck with half a million people gathered around in the streets for many hours, dancing, singing, and drinking. This atmosphere is difficult to achieve in a theatre setting where audiences are charged for entry as it is very expensive to bring these artists on tour to the United States. Crucially, even if there are no seats in the venue, there is still a clear separation between the band on stage and the audience. At the concert, the Rio-based samba percussion group descended from the stage at the end of the night and allowed themselves to be engulfed by the crowd. The shift in energy in the space was palpable—it was as though everyone let out a deep sigh and allowed themselves to fall into more familiar patterns of dancing without any self-consciousness or separation of music from dancing, or performer from spectator.

The physical design of spaces defines how we interact. We emphasize the importance of opening up conversations about the spaces we expect dance artists in academia and the professional dance field in the United States to work in.[2] We know that we can still dance in our communities, but to gain legitimacy and its associated resources, we face barriers to entry in configurations that make it difficult to transpose our work and the value we bring. In confluent spaces, mainstream or dominant cultures are positioned as super absorbents—that is, they absorb the cultural bodies that flow through their spaces based on the assumption that everybody wants to be part of the mainstream and reap the monetary and reputational benefits of being associated with the dominant culture. Mainstream spaces like studios and stages are often presented as culturally neutral and, thus, perceived as more malleable, all-encompassing, and welcoming to anyone. This is a privileged perspective that ignores the fact that dancers across cultural forms, including both mainstream and non-mainstream forms, can cross-pollinate and influence each other. We must consider how a space can encourage or discourage this cross-pollination, and not allow the mainstream to simply absorb and dominate all who pass through.

In December 2019, Sinclair created a dance installation at The REACH, an ultramodern addition to the John F. Kennedy Center for the Performing Arts in Washington, D.C. In this creative work, Sinclair's team curated the space to be more inclusive, and they welcomed community members into their process. Located on the south side of the Kennedy Center and overlooking the Potomac River waterfront, The REACH was created to accommodate diverse and creative exploration by unconventional artists. The venue has multiple theatres for filming and dance studios for classes and rehearsals. Like most Western dance studios, the studios at The REACH are equipped with modern pianos and organs, ballet barres, marley flooring, sound-proof walls, and air conditioning and heating systems. Upon open-ing in 2019, The REACH initiative's stated purpose was to welcome artists whose works, cultures, and creative processes may not fit in the Kennedy Center's main theatre spaces. The initiative opened up the facility for visitors and tourists to walk through live rehearsals and interact with dance, music, and theatre artists during their rehearsals, creative processes, and performances.

Sinclair was selected to be the first dance artist-in-residence at The REACH's "Office Hours," a program that offered different dance artists a weeklong residency and honorarium to create an innovative work. During his residency, he created "Facets of Esoterics," a site-imposed piece, meaning that it was created in one space as an influence but could also be transposed to other locations. The piece was based on the issue of racial disparities, examining how privilege and marginaliza-tion exist within social spaces, broadly defined. He focused on how space shapes the lives of the marginalized and confines them or hinders them from being a part of the mainstream in physical, mental, and spiritual ways.

The residency involved six dancers who met for eight hours each day for a week, with open showings and conversations during the last two days. Sinclair recalls that the first time he walked into The REACH, he thought, "I could take up this space," as opposed to the restrictive feeling of, "What am I allowed to do in here?" that he usually feels when he walks into Western dance studios. Throughout his residency, he felt liberated by the idea that people did not arrive expecting a cer-tain type of performance. There was no expectation about what the creative team should be doing at any given moment. Visitors could wear whatever they wanted, sit anywhere, and behave however they wanted. Sinclair and his team set that tone and expectation by way of example. They did not treat it as a performance or a formal rehearsal where people had to be quiet but as an informal creation process that visitors could participate in.

He created three separate installations around material objects—sand, porcelain plates, and books—to create three distinct spatial designs that covertly organized how the audience would perceive and interact with that space. In the book instal-lation, for instance, they used books as an object metaphor to simulate intellectual hardship, highlighting the difficulty that Black people, including those who are highly educated, have in achieving success in American society. Sinclair based this on his time living in the Washington, D.C., area, where he found that attending schools of higher learning and reading extensively does not guarantee success in the world. The young African American performers who participated in the resi-dency responded that they felt this idea on a visceral level, and they could empa-thize with the feeling of being surrounded by large tomes cluttering the room, with their old book smell. The multisensory experience reminded them of the struggles of attending institutions of higher education and feeling like they were not good enough to be there.

Visitors streamed in and out throughout the week, so no one got a sense of the piece in its entirety. Without sensing the big picture, they latched onto small details in the spatial architecture and the props and formed their own inter-pretations around them. For example, one of Sinclair's friends interpreted the porcelain white plate installation to represent White fragility—a symbol that Sinclair did not intend, but which fit the message of the work. The looseness and openness of the space allowed people to meander, explore, and let their minds wander.

Sinclair approached his work at The REACH using a non-Western creative process, highlighting the potential for a confluence of experiences and ideas. He was not preparing for a proscenium presentation and fully had community in mind as part of his dance making process. That community might have deep knowledge of his culture or come from other cultural orientations. Whereas other artists in this situation might have felt frustrated or discouraged by people entering the studio while they were working, he appreciated the ability to keep the space open. He curated the objects in his piece with certain themes in mind but also allowed for interpretations besides his own. He was grateful to the Kennedy Center team for opening up the space in this way. The flexibility of the residency program allowed for new experiences and new ways of viewing dance from both performer and audience perspectives.

Although the studio architecture and layout were similar to other typical Western dance studios, The REACH team opened up the possibility for Sinclair to intentionally curate an experience for his visitors and collaborators. By allowing people to stream in and out of the creative space, his team resisted becoming absorbed by the mainstream aesthetics that the space could have demanded of them. Sinclair felt the free flow of ideas and movements, unhindered by expectations and restrictions. The space allowed for the possibility of more fully expressing himself. In the following section, we discuss another creation process for a collaborative piece that was meant to be just as open and flexible but, in execution, noticeably collided with the expectations of Western performance. We reflect on why this happened and why different people responded in various ways.

Cultural migrations and transpositions

In this section, we share our migratory experiences of being in spaces outside of our dance cultures and our feelings of discomfort and alienation in mainstream dance spaces in the United States. As dancers, such migrations involve transpositions of cultural expressions from one space to another and require deep knowledge of both cultures to successfully convey the significance of a dance in a new context. We see cultural transpositions in dance as the mapping of movements and values from one space to a new space with a different cultural orientation. Linguists Dickins, Hervey, and Higgins use the term cultural transposition to examine challenges in linguistic translation, arguing that translation between two languages involves a transfer of one culture to another in a process that is much more challenging than simply translating linguistic differences (2017). As we described in Chapter 1, we see language as a helpful way to understand dance, but only to a point, and this notion of cultural transposition points to the limitations of simple linguistic translation when placing the semantics of a dance culture (and not just its vocabulary) into a new space. Cultural transposition involves knowledge of one's own cultural meanings and values, as well as the ability to adapt these meanings and values to different spatial contexts and configurations.

We have found that the ease with which cultural transpositions take place can be either mitigated or inhibited by academic leadership, arts administrators, artistic directors, and funders who determine what is valuable in dance and what should be elevated, funded, and prioritized. In the dialogue that follows, we discuss challenges of cultural transposition that we faced in a creative collaboration that we worked on together, in order to point to the need for what we refer to as "curatorial reeducation" in mainstream performance spaces in the United States. As we navigate cultural confluences as dancers from non-mainstream forms, we take on the responsibility of curating our own spaces while also educating audiences about the value of our forms. We point to particular spatial elements in this collaboration that either supported or impeded our work and how different people experienced the spaces that we curated. Our conversation reflects our experiences as educators, creators, and collaborators.

***

Case study dialogue: Cultural confluences in a community-based dance collaboration

In 2020–2021, the two of us collaborated with Brazilian musician Pablo de Oliveira on a creative residency project entitled, "Ainihi e Alteridade: Performing Otherness,"[3] which was funded by NextLOOK, offered through a partnership between The Clarice at the University of Maryland and Joe's Movement Emporium in Mt. Rainier, MD. The residency took place at Joe's Movement Emporium in October 2021 and explored how audiences perceive the "Othered" body through rhythms and movements drawn from Nigerian, Brazilian, and Irish cultures. This project provided the original impetus for this book, and early conversations about confluent spaces arose from our experience of trying to bring together our three ostensibly disparate cultural expressions in a performance venue in the D.C. area. We challenged ourselves to structure a performance event that felt "true" to the cultural contexts we were drawing from but also addressed the issues that come with translation, transposition, and transplantation when uprooting a cultural tradition from its home or original context. The work was an exploration of confluent spaces—culturally expressive bodies moving across various diasporic borders within a shared performance space. Through this project, we guided participants in our residency to access the space of the "Other."

Like Sinclair's residency at the Kennedy Center's REACH, the NextLOOK program gave us the freedom to use a Western performance space however we wanted. We sought to bring together multiple cultural expressions and communities, which meant creating a physical space for cultural confluences and also inviting people who themselves brought their own migratory experiences into the space. In this residency, our purpose was to experiment with how much we could strip away the idea of "performance" or "presentation" to engage in a process that felt closer to the work we do in our respective dance communities. We were in residency in a theatre space within Joe's Movement Emporium for one week and presented a "creative gathering" at the end of the week for friends and guests to participate in. We were clear that even though the event was in a theatre, it was not a performance but, rather, a social event in which everyone was invited to dance with us and play the percussion instruments we provided for them. There was no stage, but the room had a clear performance area where a curtain cordoned off one-quarter of the room from the rest. The sound and light controls were on the other side of the performance area. We tried to ignore this separation by placing musicians in front of the curtain while we danced behind, in front of, and around them. We decided to forego theatre lighting and instead borrowed portable lighting from friends to softly illuminate the entire room. In terms of "human infrastructure," we filled the space with music and dance collaborators from our cultures whom we respect and whom we knew would bring their years of training into the process to help us create something meaningful.

Our residency was received with mixed feedback. As we describe in the dialogue that follows, our process with "Ainihi e Alteridade" demonstrates what happens when cultural confluences are embraced by some but ignored or misunderstood by others. We created a multicultural space of diverse cultural expressions, and some experienced a sense of community and enjoyment because they were encouraged to bring their own cultural knowledge to the event. Others, on the other hand, expected a show and felt disappointed, disconnected, and unimpressed.

Sinclair: The idea for this residency project came out of our samba party encounter at the pizza restaurant that we describe in the opening of this book. When I first walked into Pablo's music event that night, the space felt so familiar to me, even though the language was different. I felt compelled to reach out to you two to propose working together on something. Brazil and Nigeria are 7,164 km apart, and the dance and music customs of each country are absolutely different. But it was the way the space was configured, with people eating, drinking, talking, dancing, and singing along, that drew me in and made me feel a cultural connection. There is a relationship between Afro-Brazilian music and the Yoruba people of Nigeria, but this project wasn't meant to engage directly with this particular link, in part because I am Urhobo, not Yoruba. We weren't trying to prove any kind of concrete historical connection between our cultural expressions, but our goal with this project was more abstract. We wanted to experiment with what would happen when the three of us—you, me, and Pablo—and our other collaborators from various traditions (Ghanaian dance, Afro-Cuban drumming, American jazz, Afrobeat, Appalachian dance, etc.) gathered in a room together, as people and as artists who connected over having felt alienated in mainstream performance spaces here in the United States.

Kate: Even though we come from such different cultures, we all felt inspired by each other. I remember the first time we gathered in the residency space to move together. It was a nice confluence of cultures because we didn't set any expectations about what a final product was supposed to look like. You taught me some Urhobo and Tiv steps, and you responded to Pablo's Brazilian music based on how it made you feel. I remember there was one song that felt very lively and energetic to me, mostly because I knew the upbeat *forró* dance that would normally be danced to it, but you said, "Ah, this is exactly the Hausa rhythm!" and proceeded to do some slow and slinky movements. It was interesting to note our different interpretations of the music based on our cultural dispositions. Also, we hadn't originally planned to include any of my Irish dancing since it felt so disconnected from the link between Nigeria and Brazil, but I was inspired in the moment by the 6/8 rhythms that our Brazilian and Ghanaian drummers were playing. It sounded similar to the Irish jig rhythm that is also in 6/8, so we added that in at some point, which I think added a nice, if not curious, new element to the work.

Sinclair: It is amazing to think that we created an evening-length dance work with steps from almost all regions and groups in Nigeria, including Hausa, Igbo, Yoruba, Urhobo, Benin, Tiv, and more, to almost all Brazilian songs, and danced full routines to Ghanaian drumming with a mixture of Irish steps and more. This was a really hard task, and I think we surprised ourselves with how fluid, flexible, expressive, freeing, engaging, and creative it felt to us all. It felt very different from the pressures I usually feel when creating in a theatre space.

Kate: One thing that I remember on the night of our creative gathering, after the four preceding days in residency, was how it felt like we were still in creation mode. Even though there was an audience—most of whom danced with us while others sat and watched—we didn't act like we were on stage. We didn't have an exact start time. We just let people wander in while we also meandered around until people gathered and generated enough energy to start. The evening didn't have the typical start, climax, and end, but the energy fluctuated throughout. I had some moments of mild panic when I looked around and didn't see you anywhere, but you had just gone to the back of the room to get some water and chat with a friend. We weren't all waiting backstage for our turn in the spotlight like we usually would in a proscenium performance. I also remember that we would all be dancing together in a circle and just as the energy was building up, you would drop your hand into the middle and then walk away, which somehow, we all knew to follow. I understood that this was like a "reset" or a chance to catch our breath. I could tell that some spectators were confused by this sudden reset just when things got going because they had been expecting a fully rehearsed, continuous performance, perhaps with some virtuosic dancing thrown in.

Sinclair: Yes! When I put my hand in the middle—this is a cultural cue in Nigerian communities that the leader uses to encourage a movement.

He then looks out for fatigue among the dancers and then signals an end of that dance sequence so the energy doesn't overwhelm everyone. Doing this meant that I was responding and adapting to how the participants were feeling, not just forging ahead with a performance because of the expectation that we keep entertaining.

Kate: I actually felt some anxiety when we suddenly stopped dancing because, since we were in a performance venue, I did feel that expectation to perform. I am so used to "putting on a show" and showing off my training as a dancer, and I had to consciously put aside those anxieties throughout the process. We were very intentional about trying to resist what that kind of space seemed to be demanding of us. The tech team at the venue also insisted on putting out rows of chairs in front of where the musicians were sitting, which set up a situation in which some people felt they had to sit and watch a performance. We would have preferred to just have chairs along the periphery in case someone couldn't stand for long periods of time or wanted to sit down and take a break. But the idea was that most would participate. Some people understood that they were meant to dance and play music, but others sat down and watched, which was also fine. But some looked a little uncomfortable and unsure about what was going on. I kept thinking about how they were judging us, but I was also proud of us for pushing ahead to use the space in this way.

Sinclair: Another way that we subverted expectations was that we paid people $10 when they walked in the door, rather than charging them to enter. In my traditional Urhobo customs, the host usually provides welcoming gifts like water, alcohol, kola nuts for libations, and so on. Visitors are welcome to bring what they have but should not insinuate that the host has nothing to offer. The offering of gift items is a normal part of cultural events where I come from. Offering $10 to audience members as they walked into the venue flipped the capitalist script on what people expect at a performance. In fact, paying them indicated not only that they were our guests, but also that this was not a performance, and they were invited to join us in making music and dancing. Originally, we wanted to offer food and drinks as well, but we couldn't because of COVID-19 restrictions.

Kate: People seemed pleasantly surprised to be given even a small token. This gesture signaled to them that it was an informal social space that was as much theirs as it was ours. Our main collaborators also appreciated the informality of the process. One of the American jazz musicians who participated in the residency said, "We need to do this again but at other venues. This is what Western musicians should learn to do more of, to see that we can share dance and music freely without the pressure to perform." We also left it ambiguous as to who was leading the event. Was it Pablo with his Brazilian music or was it you with your Nigerian dancing? It felt easy and natural because we allowed the cultural confluences to happen without forcing a connection or trying to justify our collaboration in so-called "intellectual" terms, which is something I struggle with.

Sinclair: That is true, but what we created wasn't just for creation's sake. We intended for some real-life positive effects to occur. One of the dancers who participated, a young African American modern dancer, got really emotional at one point. She commented to me about the joy that was happening in the space while, at the same time, she realized for the first time how our brothers and sisters in the diaspora have been feeling for all these years trying to navigate the American cultural system. Being exposed to this joy made her realize the immense cultural deprivation that she didn't know she had, and she left wanting more experiences like this one.

Kate: That is so powerful and exactly the kind of outcome we hoped for. I talked to people who didn't fully understand what was going on and didn't know how to respond, but they recognized the presence of specific cultural cues. After the event, one of my friends who was there said, "I felt like I was experiencing culture." I was intrigued by this comment because he didn't say "a" culture or any particular culture, but just spoke about the idea of culture in general. He grew up in Central America, so even though he didn't know Brazilian, Nigerian, or Irish cultures specifically, he had experienced the kind of migration and cultural transposition that we were exploring in this work. Due to his own experience of cultural confluences, he recognized that something was going on, even if he didn't understand it completely.

Sinclair: That shows a certain kind of cultural preparation and openness to something new. Rather than judging it negatively because he didn't understand every detail, he could appreciate that a lot was going on that was significant. Even we, as the lead collaborators, didn't fully understand every detail of the cultures that were in the space. For example, I didn't know what was going on with your feet during the Irish dancing part, and all of the Nigerian rhythms and movements that I brought were completely new to you.

Kate: Right! It was also hard for me to be okay with not understanding everything and feeling in control. I think some audience members were uncomfortable with how loose it felt. Some expected a performance, despite how we promoted it. One person who is a leader in the D.C. arts community came and they remained seated and browsed on their phone for most of the event. They asked us afterward, "What *was* that?" and asked if we actually had a creative process. This person said it just seemed like a "little spontaneous dance jam" in a tone that suggested that we put no effort or intention into the event and there was no technique or rigor to our process. In fact, preparing for this residency took us over two years of deliberations, conversations, and writing, from the initial proposal in early 2019 to the residency week itself in late 2021, after being postponed twice due to COVID-19. I was surprised that someone who did not participate and did not even fully pay attention could pass such a harsh judgment.

Sinclair: It was so disappointing but not surprising. As an African dancer in the United States, I have experienced this kind of comment many times. We may have stripped away the Western idea of performance so much that we removed what was familiar to this individual. Also, we did not incorporate the signs that arise from touristic and colonial stereotypes that signal when something is foreign or exotic. We were dressed in our everyday clothes, so maybe the performance itself didn't look like anything special. Maybe they wanted us to wear grass skirts or something. Our choreography was simple, and that was because we wanted people to follow along and dance with us. Maybe the way we configured the space did not fulfill their fantasies about what we should do. In any case, it was either too familiar or not familiar enough to this individual, and thus the event became illegible to them. The translation from their expectation of a performance to this more participatory event was too much for them to process. This comment was a classic erasure of the work we had put into this project, and throughout our lives as artists, because this individual could not see or understand its value.

Kate: We tried to make it clear that our "spontaneous little dance jam" was extremely intentional when we spoke briefly between each song and in the post-event dialogue that we had with participants at the conclusion of the gathering. Our intentionality largely came into play when we specifically invited friends who we knew would "get it" and would participate in culturally appropriate ways, and they did. Our approach shifted the focus to people, trusting that the dancers and audience would bring with them their own experiences and would shape the space in a particular way. That means that we were shifting the responsibility in part to the community, instilling trust in them, and allowing the event to develop organically without exerting total control over it as the "producers" of the event (or the "choreographers" or "directors" or "composers").

Sinclair: Exactly. When we talk about intentionality, it is not necessarily about making a detailed floor plan with tons of diagrams and spreadsheets to illustrate our "intentions" for the event. Spatial design is one thing, but spatial curation is another. When transposing to a new space, you always have to till the ground first before achieving the desired outcome. For us, the process was about conversations and identifying people whom we wanted to share the space with. We also left some "rough edges" visible during the event—like not having a backstage area and drinking water or changing shoes in full view. But these were only "rough" if you looked at the event from the perspective of Western theatrical aesthetics. For us, it smoothed out the edges that can be so jarring when working in a space that is not built for us. That one person's comment diminished the cultural process of people like us, who are trying to use our own languages and practices to bring together communities that have been scattered all over the United States due to various circumstances. Feeling connected to other people and making this art more accessible should be enough.

Kate: It's always the more negative comments that stick with us, but I think it's important to remember that this person's feedback was a part of the process that we envisioned. Any positive and negative responses that we got in the ensuing weeks were all a part of the research experiment that we had planned out. We often feel pressured to focus on the product—an upcoming performance that needs to be polished, leaving no time for conversations, wandering, or "play." Our goal here was to make "play" and process the entire purpose.

Sinclair: We have to keep pushing to create spaces where this kind of play can happen. And a dance space is never a sterile laboratory, it's a social and cultural space filled with contradictions. As professional artists, we will always be up against the power dynamics of being paid for our work, and, going back to our conversations about aesthetics, we have to meet expectations about what our work should look like. But we also think about the expectations that our communities have of our work. In the end, we have to push forward to implement spatial reconfigurations that allow us to work on our own terms and those of our dance communities.

***

Conclusion

In this chapter, we have examined geographical sites of confluence; the spatial design of physical structures; and the body as a surface that accumulates and expresses cultural confluences through performance. Our process in "Ainihi e Alteridade: Performing Otherness" exemplifies what we envision for our field. As utopian as it may seem, we want to see more creative processes in which cross-cultural streams come together in a natural exchange of ideas, where artists connect, build on each other, and make discoveries together. Hearing both positive and negative reactions to the process taught us that we cannot take for granted the people who understand what it means to participate in the creation and sharing of different cultural expressions. We learned that those who have experienced cultural migrations in their lives are often the most receptive to the kind of experience we offered.

In the following chapter, we examine processes for creating, performing, and practicing dance that may differ from the Western mainstream. We consider the role of so-called "steps" in dance-making through choreography and improvisation, and, in particular, the racialized implications of calling one's creative process "just an improvisational dance jam." We build on our discussions about language, aesthetics, and space to examine words and attitudes that diminish the value of creative processes in traditional dance forms as non-intellectual. Further, we examine how the apparent repeatability of dance steps lends legitimacy to a form, and how dance steps frame one's relationship to tradition, on the one hand, and contemporaneity, on the other.

Notes

1 For more about the differences between stage frevo and street frevo, see Spanos (2019) and Spanos and Bezerra (2020).
2 We are aware that federal, state, and local zoning laws require that indoor spaces, including dance studios and theatres, meet certain conditions. Governmental systems largely shape the ways we dance in different environments in the United States.
3 The word *ainihi* means "identity" in Hausa and *alteridade* means "alterity" or "otherness" in Portuguese.

References

Achebe, Chinua. 2009. *The Education of a British-Protected Child: Essays*. New York, NY: Alfred A. Knopf.

"Contact Zone." n.d. Oxford Reference. Accessed June 23, 2022. https://doi.org/10.1093/oi/authority.20110803095634533.

Davida, Dena, ed. 2011. *Fields in Motion: Ethnography in the Worlds of Dance*. Waterloo, Ontario: Wilfrid Laurier University Press.

Dickins, James, Sándor G. J. Hervey, and Ian Higgins. 2017. "Cultural Transposition." In *Thinking Arabic Translation: A Course in Translation Method*, Second edition, 29–39. Thinking Translation Series. London, UK: Routledge.

Feld, Steven. 1996. "Waterfalls of Song: An Acoustemology of Place Resounding in Bosavi, Papua New Guinea." In *Senses of Place*, edited by Steven Feld and Keith H. Basso, 91–135. Santa Fe, NM: School of American Research Press.

Feld, Steven, and Keith H. Basso, eds. 1996. *Senses of Place*. Santa Fe, NM: School of American Research Press.

Foster, Susan Leigh. 2019. *Valuing Dance: Commodities and Gifts in Motion*. New York, NY: Oxford University Press. https://doi.org/10.1093/oso/9780190933975.001.0001.

Solomon, Thomas. 2000. "Dueling Landscapes: Singing Places and Identities in Highland Bolivia." *Ethnomusicology* 44: 257–80.

Spanos, Kathleen A. 2019. "A Dance of Resistance from Recife, Brazil: Carnivalesque Improvisation in Frevo." *Dance Research Journal* 51 (3): 28–46. https://doi.org/10.1017/S0149767719000305.

Spanos, Kathleen A., and Amilcar Almeida Bezerra. 2020. "Dancing between Pedagogy and Performance: Guerreiros Do Passo and the Case of Brazilian Frevo." *Dance Chronicle* 43 (1): 3–31. https://doi.org/10.1080/01472526.2019.1708141.

4   Choreography, improvisation, and "just steps"

Interlude by Kate: Grounding an identity in steps

That was a nice dance … but what was it about?

This has always been a difficult question for me to answer as an Irish dancer. If someone asks me what my steps "mean," I do not have a concrete answer. The question makes me feel inadequate, as though the steps that I have been doing for most of my life are meaningless, rote exercises with no artistry. Especially as I have navigated dance in academia in the United States, I have felt pressure to add "meaning" or theatricality in order to legitimize my practice. This pressure, in my view, comes from the hierarchization of contemporary dance forms over so-called traditional or folk dances, and it often makes me feel that I do not belong in the same spaces where modern or contemporary dance is primarily taught and performed. I feel immense pride in my identity as an Irish dancer, but I also admit to feeling some sense of shame, as though I am not quite a "real dancer." As much as I have learned to embrace who I am as a dancer over many years, the insecurities linger. I started taking jazz and modern classes in high school, in part because I felt that I needed to learn how to do *pliés* and *chainé* turns to fill perceived gaps in my training and meet unspoken expectations about how to be a dancer. Although I enjoy these forms, they have never fully captivated me the way Irish dancing has.

I would say that Irish dance has a vocabulary and a syntax, a logic as to how steps connect. But when I dance, I am not telling a story or even addressing a larger theme. When I make up new steps, I build from a toolkit of movements that I find pleasing. The combinations may have a delightful rhythmic variation or a new move that I have been working on, not connected to a narrative storyline or larger idea.

I am not saying that there is no art or emotion in Irish dance, which is often seen as exceedingly rigid, with arms stuck to the sides and blank facial expressions. Although the dance posture looks rigid, I feel free when I dance. When I was younger, I enjoyed the pure joy of leaping in the air, jumping higher than I thought I could, or stamping frustrations out on the floor after a bad day. Now that I'm older, I often find myself moved to tears when I dance even my simplest

DOI: 10.4324/9781003231226-5

beginner steps. There is something comforting about their familiarity, as well as my continued effort to perfect them. Sometimes my days working in an office are so disembodied, and, for me, Irish dancing feels like coming home. Some of these steps have accompanied me for most of my life. My body just knows them. They are comforting, and the exercise releases something chemical and emotional due to the sweating, accelerated heart rate, and heavy breathing.

I spoke once with an academic colleague who is a modern dance practitioner about this experience. I explained how I feel my thinking brain shut off when I get into the flow of the dance and how I feel fully present in my active body when mus- cle memory takes over. They responded with a mixture of curiosity and disdain: "Oh, I am *always* thinking when I dance," as though my experience was merely physical and lacking an intellectual component. I wondered: What does it mean to think when you dance? Beyond the physiological, I feel that my steps carry vast amounts of valuable cultural knowledge and connect me to my own personal history, as well as others who also share these steps. Even if a step itself does not tell a story, stories are central to the transmission of traditional dance and music. Knowing "who taught who" a step or tune is a crucial piece of information. Also, is there no intellect in the body itself, outside of the brain? When I dance my steps with their set patterns, I can feel my whole body anticipating each movement. I also feel engaged with an archive of other bodies thinking in this same pattern, and I feel my body telling our stories with each step.[1] For me, the steps convey and pro- duce meaning as I perform them. There is no meaning separate from that particular moment of embodiment that I have to articulate.

In some ways, I have used dance throughout my life to quiet my tendency to overthink. Early on in my competitive training, I used Irish dance to discipline my body and calm my mind. I approached my steps as a mathematical exercise that always had a right answer. There was no gray area about what was right or wrong in terms of being rhythmically on time, having proper technique, memo- rizing pre-choreographed steps, and creating steps to fit neatly into the melodic grid of the music or floor patterns based on geometric symmetry. That sense of control and discipline was comforting amidst the anxieties of my teenage years and early twenties. However, my relationship with Irish dance started to change after I retired from competition and began to study the history of Irish dance in more depth. I learned the idea that disciplining bodies through the dance was part of Ireland's resistance against British colonization in the late-nineteenth and early twentieth centuries, to show how "proper" and "disciplined" the Irish could be and challenge discriminatory portrayals of the Irish as lazy, unruly, and backward (Brennan 2001). But I also learned how so-called "traditional" Irish dances were "invented" (as in the process described by Hobsbawm and Ranger [1983]) by "men in suits" (to quote Dunne [2022]) and placed within the strictures of Ireland's na- tionalist movement, which resulted in writing out many other local dance styles and forms from the official narrative (Cullinane 1987; Brennan 2001; Foley 2001, 2011, 2012a, 2013, 2021). I did not learn about these local styles and techniques in depth until I went to Ireland to study. The experience changed my perspective on what Irish dance could be and taught me that I did not have to stay boxed into one rigid style. Instead, I found that there was room for me to discover my own expression and softness in a variety of styles.

I see this realization as related to my diaspora experience, growing up half-Irish American in the United States and going to Ireland as an adult to study at the University of Limerick. I was surprised by how free Irish dance and music felt there and how open to innovation and experimentation the Master's program was.[2] We focused equally on traditional and modern Irish dance and so-called theatrical, or contemporary, choreography. Both were difficult in their own ways—the former for its strict standards of technique and historical stylings and the latter for its methodologies in experimental artmaking. But I never had to justify why I was using Irish dance vocabulary. The experience gave me a sense of what it feels like to be a dancer whose foundational training isn't questioned.

However, I did face difficulties with my identity as an American abroad in Ireland. While I felt at home with my dance language because I knew the steps, I felt like my Americanness was a large presence and took up a lot of space. I tried to make myself smaller to make up for it and felt myself become even quieter and more insecure than usual. After a few months, I learned the phrase "trying to out-Paddy the Paddy," referring to Irish Americans who try too hard to prove their Irishness. I became self-conscious about how much I identified with a country that I did not grow up in, even though I had shaped my identity around being an Irish dancer. Coming home to the United States was even more difficult because I felt boxed in again. I had to either (1) provide an extensive explanation and justification for using Irish dance vocabulary in mainstream dance spaces, which were predominated by ballet, modern, and contemporary dancers; or (2) remain within the rigid confines of Irish dance "tradition" as it is defined in Irish American circles. With the latter, I ran up against a lot of resistance to doing anything even slightly outside of the box. I felt out of place in either scenario. This is the crux of my migratory experience as an Irish dancer.

Throughout all of this, I have always felt grounded by the steps that have traveled with me as I have moved through various spaces, and that is why I care so much about them. Although the steps themselves may not mean anything, they become meaningful as I do them. As Irish dance choreographer Colin Dunne says, "Forms are not expressive in themselves. People are expressive" (2022). The value of these steps is embodied in the dancers who carry the tradition with them throughout their lives and adapt it along the way.

***

The value of "just steps"

"What is it about?" is a key question that both of us have had to deal with as dancers practicing non-mainstream forms in the United States. The problem is not that our steps do not have meaning. They do. Rather, it is that we have to explain what they mean in terms that are considered acceptable within institutional spaces. As described in Chapter 2, academic dance spaces in the United States largely promote a particular set of Western aesthetic values. We have found that, whether we use simple terms to describe our dances or present a full structural analysis in terms that are meaningful to us—such as a rhythmic breakdown of an Irish hornpipe step or the highly polyrhythmic Urhobo *Ema* dance—we are told by professors and colleagues that our analysis is either insufficient or too tedious. This scrutiny is different from constructive criticism or critique, which is when a person brings their own value to help uplift the work, which we fully welcome. Instead, these demands devalue our dance traditions on an institutional level, making us doubt our merit as artists and discouraging us from sharing our cultures.

Dance is never "just dance." Cultural codes permeate all dance forms, even if some seem to transcend cultural markings. Dance scholar Henrietta Bannerman explains that some cultural codes in dance involve "sophisticated forms of mime" and gesture in choreography (which she identifies in classical ballet and classical Indian dances), whereas other dance cultures rely on a combination of contextual elements such as music, costuming, food, and social cues along with movement and gesture that convey meaning (2014, 68–69). The problem we see is that some dances appear to have too much culturally specific coding, so to speak, and that coding must be translated in ways that are understood in mainstream spaces in the United States (as described in Chapter 1). Consider a b-boy spinning on the street, a flatfooter shuffling on a porch, a femme queen duckwalking in a ballroom competition, two teenagers whining at the dance hall, or even a TikToker posting the latest dance challenge. All of these dances are more than "just dance" and involve codes that tell us something about a person and their culture, even if the story is not immediately discernible by gesture alone.

We have both been told that our steps are "meaningless" or "not intellectual enough" in academic dance circles precisely because they are associated with frameworks from traditional cultures, as though we are simply mimicking the steps of others that came before us and not thoughtfully engaging with them. We have also encountered a certain resistance to codified steps or vocabulary from our traditions and have been told to focus instead on abstraction and the individual improvisational body. Abstraction is sometimes a way to make our work more digestible and comfortable for outsiders because it does not require additional education to understand the culture. That is, our work would be more contemporary if we avoided codified steps with names (any step that is so embedded in the tradition that it is known by a recognized name), and invented new movement patterns instead, abstracting them from their cultural context. While we are not opposed to this kind of creative innovation, citing dancers from our past and present communities by activating specific steps is what gives our dances significance and shows respect to those dancers. When we cannot call the community into the space through these kinesthetic references, our steps become diluted and lose their meaning. The effect of this bias, in both of our experiences in academic programs focused on modern or postmodern dance, is to place less value on non-mainstream dance forms that *do* have recognizable or codified steps, as though adherence to tradition means less intellectual or creative engagement.

In our experiences, including our "Ainihi e Alteridade" collaboration described in Chapter 3, such devaluing is often centered around the word "just" ("just a spontaneous jam," "just a playful little dance"), which diminishes our practices to meaningless or useless activity. Dance scholar Brenda Dixon-Gottschild points out that African diasporic dances, for example, have been perceived as "not 'real choreography' ... but simply steps strung together" (1998, 53). The idea of "simply steps strung together" suggests that these dances are only about the physicality of recreational movement—just dancing to sweat or have fun. The underlying assumption that these dances are only about physicality implies that they are unsuitable for the concert stage or serious intellectual pursuit, as though one cannot do all of these things at once. Neither of us identifies as being from the African diaspora, but we both find resonance in Dixon-Gottschild's observation. Her concern relates to other dances that have been pejoratively classified as mere "folk" dances for their lack of technique or rigor, on the one hand, and their status as virtuosic and exotic "spectacles," on the other. Reducing dance forms to "just" steps, or scrutinizing practices as simply fun, playful, or providing the physiological release that Kate describes in the opening of this chapter, undercuts the deep value and nuance to be found in these modalities. In Chapter 1, we discussed how value in dance as an art form has been partly determined based on how "serious" or "playful" a dance appears to be. This chapter continues that conversation in the specific context of creating steps and meaning in traditional dance. "Playful" dances are just as valuable, but different dance cultures require specific terminology to express that value. Here, we describe how our so-called "just steps" in Irish and Nigerian dances are sites packed with cultural knowledge, emotion, and storytelling.

Throughout this chapter, we use the terms "traditional" or "folk" dance to refer to a specific type of dance that has been identified as representative of a culture and to demonstrate how we locate value in our own so-called traditional or folk dance steps. Perhaps the reason that an obsession with steps comes up so much in traditional dance forms is that the very idea of tradition suggests that the dance is formed around a catalog of steps, movements, and rhythms that carry meaning over generations. These dance forms and their steps may be practiced as part of the lived experience of a community or as part of a revival movement (Buckland 1983; Nahachewsky 2001), or they may have been codified and formalized in some way to transmit that culture through movement. Both of us see tradition as a dynamic and fluid process,[3] but we also believe that, in practice, this fluidity is difficult to maintain because the borders of a particular "tradition" and ownership are so often contested, even among our own communities. In addition, steps do not have to be written down in order to be codified and considered traditional. In African dance, for example, Sinclair recognizes how songs, movements, and customs have been codified to give meaning to particular activities. Those steps are encoded and transmitted through spoken native languages, not written down. Keeping in mind that many traditional dance forms are documented in ephemeral ways, we wonder: What is the relationship between an individual, a community, and a tradition in determining what steps are valuable?

In this chapter, we use the examples of modern, postmodern, and the broad category of "contemporary" dance in the United States as a counterpoint to traditional dances, or dances with perceived strong cultural markings and histories. Both of us have often been confronted with the idea in the United States that modern or postmodern dance is neutral and lacks any cultural baggage. We want to emphasize that we are not singling out modern or postmodern dance as inherently exclusionary or encompassing faulty methodologies, but we are highlighting the system that allows these forms to continue to escape cultural, racial, or ethnic markings. We must articulate how we create value through the creative processes that we practice in our own dance cultures because, although we do not expect everyone to enjoy every type of dance, acceptance of more diverse cultural representation that allows dancers to present their value on their own terms will enrich our field.

Finally, we examine the role that race plays in marginalizing certain dance forms to the non-mainstream in our framework of cultural confluences. It is important to clarify here the subtle difference between the terms "marginalized" and "non-mainstream" and how we deploy them in this chapter. Here, marginalization relates to the intentional and systematic exclusion of one group by another group in power, which is very different from the ways that we have talked about mainstream and non-mainstream as having constantly shifting borders, sometimes flowing naturally in and out of each other in various global contexts. In particular, we examine how dance steps and creative processes arising from marginalized forms have been historically devalued in racial terms, as well as how Whiteness has become unmarked and monolithic in our field. As we discuss in the following dialogue, choreography and improvisation have been generalized and racialized as "White" and "Black" approaches to dance creation, respectively, throughout dance history. This racialization affects how the two of us navigate our field as dancers and scholars.

Dialogue: Choreography, improvisation, and the racialization of dance creation practices

Conversations about the meaning of "just steps" relate specifically to the ways that dance has been conceptualized as a means of narrative storytelling, on the one hand, or abstract expression, on the other. Classical ballet choreographies feature codified gestures that are used in a narrative choreographic structure intended to follow a specific storyline, whereas modern and postmodern dance tend to embrace abstract expression and frequently break the formal rules of posture and positioning defined by ballet technique. As dance historian Susan Manning explains in *Modern Dance, Negro Dance*, abstract expression in modern dance is rooted in the context of intellectualism and racialization in the United States throughout the twentieth century, during which a push for "mythic abstraction staged universal subjects without the mediation of bodies marked as culturally other" (2004, 118). Manning demonstrates how dance critics in the mid-twentieth century recognized that racism had created biases about Black dance forms, but they did not yet recognize to what extent these biases had structured preconceptions about modern dance as well (2004, 168). That is, they did not see how Whiteness was also being defined through its lack of cultural markers in modern dance. These attitudes represent early examples of how modern and postmodern dance in predominantly White spaces have been able to embrace fluid vocabularies of individual expression that, on the surface, seem to transcend race, ethnicity, and culture.

Modern dance does not have a monopoly on abstraction, however. Most, if not all, dance cultures implement abstraction to some extent. If we strip away the racial, ethnic, and cultural markings of some traditional dances, the steps that are left are quite abstract when isolated and taken out of context. If we look at modern or postmodern dance with an ethnographic eye (à la Kealiinohomoku [1972, 1983]) and take into consideration their particular cultural contexts in academia or art dance, the movements can be just as "exotic" and puzzling to outsiders. In particular, the tropes of repetition and pedestrian gesture in postmodern choreographies can be difficult to discern for those not initiated in this particular dance culture, but this work is rarely interpreted through a racial, ethnic, or cultural lens. Dance scholar Rebecca Chaleff draws on both Dixon-Gottschild and Manning to argue that postmodern dance aesthetics have "perpetuated the whiteness of high modernism by twisting the trope of racial exclusion from a focus on trained bodies to a focus on ordinary bodies" (2018, 72). She examines "task-based" methods in postmodern dance choreography (i.e., choreography that is based on a series of repetitive and pedestrian movements) and shows how choreographers have participated in a "passive absenting of race," with the assumption that the White body is "ordinary" or neutral, and thus not racialized (2018, 76). The issue here, for us, again, is the assumption that White bodies performing postmodern dance aesthetics are not participating in a "cultural" performance, because both their skin color and the aesthetics they express are White.[4] These dancers and dances are cultural, of course, and they arise from the confluence of many cultures which go unnoticed and uncredited when they become absorbed into the dominant, mainstream culture. It is critical that we not only recuperate the contributions of the historically marginalized, as in Dixon-Gottschild's work, but also that we are aware of this constant cultural flow in the dance spaces that we occupy and how it affects our own identities. We remain unconvinced that repetitive postmodern "tasks" differ substantially from the traditional dance "steps" that are repeated over generations just because the latter are tied to culture and the former, ostensibly, are not. The repetition of any step or task becomes dramatized or meaningful over time—this is especially true as a dancer intentionally plays with rhythm and other stylistic variations that translate into familiar behavioral patterns.

If a White dancer performing a "postmodern task" is seen as neutral, how is that same task expressed by a dancer of color? In her article, Chaleff quotes choreographer Gerald Casel as saying, "… there is no such thing as pure movement for dancers of color" (2018, 79), to describe the experience of many throughout the history of modern dance in the United States. That is, a White dancer can get away with performing "pure, meaningless" task-based movement, whereas a dancer of color cannot escape profiling contingent on their skin color or how they are perceived to move differently from White dancers. As one of Kate's colleagues of color stated in a conversation responding to Casel's statement, "A dancer of color can never fully 'complete' the postmodern dance task," whereas, by virtue of their skin color, White dancers are never questioned as to why they are on stage performing it. We expand on this point to also consider White dancers who do not perform postmodern dance tasks, but "just steps" from other dance cultures, including "White" European folk dance forms. What tends to go unacknowledged is that there is no such thing as pure movement for *any* dancer, regardless of skin color, and there should be no one dancer or dance form that can achieve "pure" movement while all the rest are subject to stereotyping, hypervisibility, and racial profiling. Thus, in this dialogue we examine not only how a dancer is judged by their skin color but also how a dance form itself is judged by its apparent cultural, racial, or ethnic markings, and how such markings of dancers and dances complicate the assumptions that shape the Western framework for understanding and valuing dance.

We want to celebrate cultural diversity but doing so requires that Whiteness not remain unmarked. Our point here is that there are dance forms besides postmodern dance that have entirely different "tasks" (in the form of repeated or codified traditional steps) and contexts in which to perform them besides the concert stage. This chapter arises from our concern with how Whiteness has become synonymous with mainstream Western forms, with little regard for the European (predominantly White) dances that fall outside of this mainstream (like Irish dance, as an example). Just as we want to encourage exploration of the heterogeneity of Black dance forms, we also want to unravel the myth of Whiteness as a monolith. We believe that this step is crucial for making progress toward achieving greater equity in the dance field so that all recognize the cultural elements that they bring into a space.

The following dialogue examines the burden that traditional dancers carry in relation to their steps. We share examples of how both of us have felt "marked" by our dance steps and postures when we wanted to fit in and also "unmarked" when we wanted to distinguish ourselves in the dance circles we navigate. We discuss questions around intellectual engagement with traditional forms and the versatility that training various dance "languages" can bring. We discuss choreographed "steps" and improvisation in traditional dance forms; the notion of being a collector of steps or a "negotiator" of dance strategies; and how these processes of dance creation have been racialized throughout history to either marginalize dancers or put them in positions of authority.

***

Sinclair: As so-called "traditional dancers," we are often asked what our steps mean. I could be doing a simple locomotory movement to get from one place to another, like jumping or whining my hips, and someone will ask me what it means. This is not necessarily a bad question, but it feels like a challenge to justify the use of the movement. In Nigeria, different groups have traditions that are used to retain cultural histories through reenactments or performances of their most valued customs. Just as insiders know their native languages, they know these histories simply by being part of the community, and they can't explain what each element means. Outsiders, on the other hand, see steps that look very abstract and have difficulty interpreting them. This even includes dances that have been commercialized for general consumption and that have been made more accessible by having their ritual elements and deeply ac-cented cultural codes broken down and diluted.

Kate: There is an extra burden of translation for traditional dancers trying to work or reach outside of their tradition. This is one instance in which I think the analogy of dance as language works. It sounds like those lo-comotory movements that you mention, which insiders just understand without really knowing how to explain them, are like conjunctions—like "and, but, or"—used to connect ideas in a movement phrase. They are totally necessary to convey meaning but not so meaningful in and of themselves. They are the connective tissue that holds things together. And yet, I believe that the cultural substance of any dance resides in our steps and movements, especially the connective ones that make sense of the dance or hold it together. I can always tell when someone has learned a couple of cool Irish dancing moves but doesn't understand the rhythmic logic of the dance or the overall posture of the body. It's not even that their dance language is accented, as much as it is like someone using slang or cultural idioms that don't quite fit the context. The sim-plest elements don't mean a lot on their own, but they contain all that cultural substance that makes the dance recognizable. When adopting a whole new aesthetic, there is even more to understand and interpret than what first meets the eye. And just like in language, the most highly trained and fluent practitioners often have the hardest time breaking down these elements for outsiders to understand because they have be-come unconscious habits.

Sinclair: The idea that someone doesn't understand dance—African, postmod-ern, or anything else—is so foreign to me. I have always wondered what there is to understand. Is the enjoyment of a dance tied to the fact that someone must understand the dance intellectually before it gains respect as an art form? My struggle here in the United States is with how foreign cultures can be debased through language that dismisses the cultural significance of the dance. For example, in asking the sim-ple question, "What was that dance about?" and following it up with phrases like "I'm confused" and "I didn't like it," we see how harm-less curiosity can quickly lead to negative judgment and criticism of the dance culture. These comments reinforce the expectation that dance as an art form should intellectually engage audiences, even if they are outsiders who know nothing about the culture.

Kate: And how do we even define intellectual engagement with a dance, when the idea of what even is intellectual is up for debate? There is a sense that some dances are more intellectually developed than others, but I believe there is a certain intellect in the body that is engaged when we do any kind of dance because dancing conveys cultural knowledge. I have heard audience members or students who did not understand a postmodern dance performance say, "This goes over my head. I'm not smart enough to understand it," and they seem ashamed. But neither of us has encountered a student furrowing their brow in confusion after seeing an African dancer or an Irish dancer, for example, and expressing shame for not understanding the performance. What makes one performance seem intellectual and another "just" steps?

Sinclair: That's true, I have noticed this too. I'm interested in how you became triggered by the conversation started by Brenda Dixon-Gottschild about "simply steps strung together," or "just steps," as we have been calling it. I didn't have the same reaction initially, and I wonder if it is because of your diasporic experience growing up in the United States and your need to connect to your family's Irish and Greek cultures. It seems like you don't want to have to justify or defend your attachment to Irish dance. There is a certain fragility and vulnerability here that I think a lot of other people also feel, as though you worry that maybe your steps actually *are* meaningless. For me, dancing is never "just steps" because it is always meaningful, so I'm wondering if you are arguing that your steps are meaningless and that we should accept that.

Kate: It's a bit of a contradiction because I do think that my Irish dancing steps are "just steps," or kind of meaningless, in that they don't have sacred or spiritual meaning for me. The steps are like little poems that don't have a lot of profound meaning, kind of like the silly poems or drawings my mom would drop in my lunchbox as a kid. But I kept those poems, just as I have held onto my steps, because they are valuable to me. They bring comfort and a sense of delight. My steps also connect me to the Irish dance history that has been passed down to me and that I have sought to learn more about. When I dance them, I am reminded of all the individuals who have shaped the tradition in intentional and unintentional ways. In this way, yes, my steps connect me to my heritage. Also, in a more physical sense, when I learn a new step, I feel a certain hunger to "get it"—to grab onto another piece of that culture, to achieve the flow, to feel the pieces connecting. Rarely am I fully satisfied because there is always more to learn, perfect, or habituate myself to, and that is why I keep doing it.

Sinclair: Could it be that you are feeling this eagerness to "get it" because you are at this diasporic point of confluence in the United States where there are so many other cultures competing for attention? Even with the fluidity that is central to our framework for cultural confluences, there are also certain ways that we can become boxed in at those intersections, especially when you become involved with cultural expressions that are very dense and specific, like Irish dance. If we were simply located in just one or another culture, we might not feel so much pressure. For example, in Nigeria, I performed in a specific traditional dance scene with the Edo State Arts Council for a couple of years. Here, dance was a way to present our identities and hold up our patriotism, histories, and cultural pride. When we traveled to national festivals to compete with other state troupes, we were never questioned about the value of our culture or why we were doing certain steps. But I feel like the United States is so much more diverse, especially the area of Washington, D.C., where we live. My Urhobo culture here is unknown. I have to teach people to make them aware of it, and that can get tiresome when people aren't open to learning. But I think we need to give ourselves credit for staying in these spaces and striving to make sense of where and who we are as dancers and culture bearers.

Kate: I think you're right that this is very typical of the diaspora or migrant experience. Before I did my Master's in Irish dance, I was perfectly content to stay in my Irish dancing bubble, but I went to Ireland because I knew I would regret it if I didn't take the opportunity while I was still young. I expected to just go, take some classes, and come back and continue my life as it was. But that experience changed everything. Not only did it give me a deeper understanding of the competitive style I already trained in, but it also gave me a broader understanding of other forms of Irish dance and introduced me to other movement cultures from around the world, like flamenco, tap, postmodern dance, contact improvisation, and capoeira. It made me start to question how these forms interact within our bodies as we engage with them over time. I came to appreciate more where I had come from and those steps that made me who I am, and I wanted to learn more about others so I could become a more fluent mover, so to speak, in various forms.

Sinclair: If you have ever been in conversation with any Nigerians, you would know that we do something very well—we can speak in many different languages at the same time, constantly switching depending on where we are or who we are talking to. Because of this, we are also very good at understanding different communication styles due to the immense diversity we have. It's a special ability to adapt and absorb all kinds of languages and cultural codes that I think is very particular to where I come from in Africa. My dancing, like my use of different languages, has benefitted from learning and exposing myself to many different movement styles. It has made me, as Westerners would say, a "stronger, more versatile dancer."

Kate: I think that ability to shift between languages and communication styles is critical to developing respect and empathy for other people. For me, dance has always been my entry point for cross-cultural communication, even more than spoken language because I was painfully shy growing up. I have always been afraid of saying something stupid, but I was never afraid of looking "dumb" while dancing, as though I could express more with my body than I could simply verbalize. I wonder about the value of being able to code-switch with the body.

I experienced profound changes when I started to branch out to other dance forms during my Master's program, which I touched on in Chapter 2 about aesthetics and kinesthetic empathy. This exploration provided the impetus for me to start studying Brazilian movement forms in depth. My experiences with capoeira and frevo taught me to accept ambiguity and ambivalence in dance and in my life more generally, because embracing those qualities was part of our training. Concepts like *malícia, malandragem,* and *munganga* (roughly translated from Brazilian Portuguese as "trickery," "cunning," and "jerry-rigging") are all about instability and dealing with the unforeseen. Also, interestingly, my training in both forms has been much less about collecting and perfecting certain steps and more about developing strategy, interaction, and improvisation. That is, my practice has been more about how to strengthen that connective tissue we were talking about before and less about the movement patterns themselves. This was a real shift from the "collector" mode I was in with my traditional Irish steps. I have become more comfortable existing in a liminal space between seriousness and play, as we discussed in Chapter 1. Now, I find freedom in that space. I thought that I would never be able to train the Irish dancer's verticality out of my body and the rigidity out of my approach to dance, but I'm finding a sort of fluidity where I can draw from various aesthetic systems when I want to. Studying Brazilian movement forms has guided my ongoing process, as a White American woman, to "decolonize" my understanding of dance and my own identity—to confront my own assumptions and to question the power structures that define value in dance, which have inhabited my body according to Western mainstream aesthetic ideals.

Sinclair: This is interesting, and I also want to point out, as a careful assumption, that as a White person, you might not have noticed how different cultural aesthetics were always circulating around you growing up in the United States. It has been a privilege for you to be able to experience other cultures by choice. For me, growing up in postcolonial Nigeria, Nigerian and European aesthetics were always very present and at odds with each other. I was always aware of how they had to be negotiated in my daily life. For example, I had to know when to use the English language and when to use Nigerian pidgin English. Now in the United States, I don't feel the distant separation between Nigerian and European cultures anymore or the need to constantly make the quick switch from one culture to another, but I do feel more like I have to accept Western culture and embrace it while my Nigerianness is overshadowed. In addition to this, I have to deal with a new racialized experience on a daily basis, as here I am immediately judged for being Black and African before people even get to know me. This puts a lot of constraints on how I can navigate confluent spaces. I don't have the freedom to do whatever I want without thinking through the implications of how I am perceived.

And those implications are different whether I am in the United States
or in Nigeria, which, again, leads to my feeling of being in this place of
"nowhere" that we've talked about throughout our book.

Kate: I hadn't thought about how I had the choice to explore these ostensibly
"oppositional" aesthetic forms and how that experience would feel liberating to me while it feels oppressive for you. It certainly has been a
privilege for me. I suppose that I also have the privilege of feeling like
I have a very clear home base in terms of my movement preferences. I
can choose when I want to venture out to try something new or safely
retreat to my comfort zone. Despite exploring other styles, I think I will
always feel most at home with Irish dance. I find myself craving the
structure and rigidity of my Irish dance training as much as what I'll
call the "anti-structure"[5] and improvisational strategies that I train in
capoeira and frevo, and I value being able to go back and forth.

Sinclair: What you just said also points to an important distinction between choreography, as a more structured approach to creating dance, and improvisation, which is less structured or maybe even "anti-structure" when it
is used to resist certain systems that may seem exceedingly rigid, oppressive, or exclusionary. These two approaches to creating movement
have been racialized throughout history. I suppose that improvisation
would be the best way to describe my culture's dancing, although that
word has always been a trigger for me because it has historically been
used to diminish Africanist forms. The truth is that improvisation (for
lack of a better word) has to do with our system of spirituality. Improvisation is the freedom that the individual has to make artistic choices in
the moment that aren't dictated by any preconceived notion of rules or
laws about how an individual should perform. The goal of these dances
is to not be repeatable, meaning that, unless there actually is a choreography (which is more common these days due to Westernization),
breaking in and out of standardized steps and their structure is totally
normal. In fact, between participants cheering and clapping, the drummers improvising, and the overall energy in the room, the dancer is
usually transported to a state in which they don't have any choice but
to "display." We use the term "display" to mean that the dancer uses all
they have to reach excellence, to give more energy than they normally
would, and to dance more than they ever could before. This is contrary
to cultures where repetition creates authority, including the kind of authority that the word "tradition" holds.

Kate: I would say that, for me, repetition is precisely what gives traditional
Irish dance steps their meaning. Until recently, I'd never thought about
repetition as relating directly to authority, but, rather, to tradition and
continuity, as something that I assumed to be a natural lineage. But it
is true that, for something to be defined as "traditional" in Irish dance,
someone had to say so with some authority, which marginalized any local practices that did not fall within that definition. I know, for example,

that *sean nós* dance and other local step dance styles were not included in the nationalist invention of so-called traditional Irish dance in the early twentieth century. And these forms are built around improvisation, not choreographed steps. In competitive step dance today, we don't learn to improvise, so I have never felt very comfortable dancing on the fly. I have always thought of music as a grid that I have to lock into, and the process is more about locking into something already created than it is about spontaneously discovering new ways to lock in. I have always been nervous to just let the music or a musician guide me in Irish dance. I prefer to just rely on that music to steady me. I wonder if this means that I feel more comfortable with an authority to guide me, rather than giving myself permission to let go.

Sinclair: I think there is an important distinction between the repetition of steps and how precise the interpretation is. In my Urhobo dances, we do repeat steps, but it is not really about whether the steps are performed precisely the same way by different individuals. Steps that are repeated are the same from a macro level, but individuals interpret them in different ways. This has made it hard for Western scholars to understand and document what exactly the steps are, I think, and maybe it seems more random than it really is according to the underlying logic. I also think it's important to clarify that, although I come from a so-called improvisational dance tradition, I don't use improvisation when I teach or perform because I've found that, if I do, people think I'm not prepared and just want to play around. My work becomes a joke. This is because improvisation has been racialized to such an extent that someone like me can't risk being accused of being unprepared. But I have also seen how modern dancers in the United States take the term improvisation seriously, and it is even a technique and method of its own in both music and dance. I find this double standard troublesome.

Kate: I had no idea about how improvisation had been racialized until I studied frevo in Brazil in 2018. I had always thought very highly of improvisation as a skill developed over years of training, and it seemed nearly unattainable for me as a competitive step dancer. When I first started training in Brazilian movement forms, capoeira specifically, I saw improvisation as a mode of resistance used in Africanist forms, as a form of protection so that the practice couldn't be pinned down or targeted. But later I learned how frevo dance, which has its origins in capoeira (de Oliveira 1985; Bastos 2018), became codified as a way to legitimize the practice and make the case that it isn't "just" improvisation but something that can be seriously trained year-round (Spanos 2019a). One frevo master, in particular, Nascimento do Passo (1936–2009), cataloged steps and created a formal teaching methodology to gain respect as a professional dancer. As a poor Black man in northeastern Brazil, he was responding to pressures from the White elite to legitimize the form and his career.[6] However, he also maintained the importance of spontaneity and dealing with the unexpected. He referred to this concept as *munganga*, which describes what you would do if you tripped or fell but managed to seamlessly incorporate that into the dance, making it seem intentional. My teacher, Otávio Bastos, was one of his students and is further developing this methodology by teaching this basic catalog of steps but encouraging us to find our own individual expression and aesthetic interpretation through improvisation and the philosophy of *munganga*. It's a liberatory approach for me because it's also changing my relationship with Irish dance, as I find myself being more playful and less self-critical. It makes me question how tradition may not only be built on repetition and codified movement, which is what I'd always been led to believe as an Irish dancer. This must be what it means for tradition to be dynamic, fluid, and process-based.

Sinclair: It is true that improvisation can create more versatility for a dancer in terms of mastery. But a more intricate issue arises when we are allowed to deviate and dance more freely, as in your frevo example. As someone who loves the privilege to be able to do what I want with dance, I find improvisation to be a gateway to personalization and a vehicle for mobility that allows me to interact with people and surrounding cultures. Really, I could dance my steps to many types of African music if I wanted to, but this would confuse non-sub-Saharan Africans. The fluid and malleable nature of African dance is still a mystery for Westerners, but it is intentional and not random. Improvisation in my culture is deliberate, but it is often misunderstood and reduced to "just" improvisation or play.

Kate: Considering this conversation from a more macro level, I find it interesting that, even though you come from a highly improvisational form, and I come from a highly choreographed form, we have both experienced this feeling of being reduced to "just steps." Whether improvised or choreographed, it seems to come down to the fact that some dances are welcome in certain spaces while others are not, and it is not as simple as drawing a line based on race or ethnicity. But I want to be cautious when I say this because I don't want to center my own experiences in light of what dancers of color have experienced. I am conscious of a long history of equating or comparing, in particular, Irish and African histories of oppression, which falls into tricky territory.[7] Case in point, I have heard some White percussive dance scholars (who are not Irish dancers) identify Africanist aesthetics in *sean nós* because it is improvisational and closer to the floor, more like shuffling than the high stepping of the step dance tradition today. I have heard some speculation that *sean nós* was influenced by African dance and music through a direct connection between Ireland and Africa. However, I have not yet seen a study that explains this or identifies which parts of Africa these influences would come from. I don't think it is out of the realm of possibility, and the idea had previously crossed my mind as well. But hearing the claim from outsiders that *sean nós* carries Africanist aesthetics strikes me as a justification to study a White dance form in this current era that is so (rightly) focused on centering non-White forms. I am not sure that something is Africanist just because it is improvisational or rhythmic and not based on codified steps.

Sinclair: It will amaze you that I don't know of any Nigerian percussive dances. In my undergraduate thesis about contemporary Nigerian dance (Emoghene 2007), I actually stumbled upon Spanish flamenco and I was so inspired that I infused it into the very last section of my performance. But outside of contemporary exploration in dance at the levels of higher education and other institutions, I never heard of people using the term "percussive dance" to describe any dance form in my country. I am sure that when Westerners see some dances—like the Tiv *Swange* dance that uses anklets and rattles, the *Asharuwa* dance of the Afizere group in Jos Plateau State, or even the *Atilogwu* dances and the *Adanma* dance of Anambra State and the *Achikoro* of the Enugu people and other eastern Nigerian states—they think they are percussive. But I am not sure if I have heard anyone in Nigeria describe them as "percussive," per se. I know that our dances are described as polyrhythmic, and they do indeed produce or echo rhythm. So, maybe this is another way that Westerners have taken this terminology and rebranded it to suit their forms. Or maybe this is a way to distinguish the dances shared by both of our continents, to discount the clear history of cross-cultural pollination in dance and music.

Kate: There is a need to talk about this history of cross-pollination, which exemplifies the complex confluences we talk about throughout this book. Many are attracted to a particular narrative about the cooperative and conflicted relationship between Irish and African people and how their cultures intermingled in the Americas. This history is what prompted my interest in the Caribbean island of Montserrat, where I did my doctoral fieldwork on the island's so-called "Afro-Irish" St. Patrick's Festival and other annual festivals (Spanos 2017, 2019b). I focused on one particular step in their national masquerade dance—the heel and toe polka—which, according to the common narrative, comes from Irish dance. Knowing that I was an Irish dancer, masquerade leaders there expected me to know the step already, and although it had some familiar motifs (heel, toe, and a little hop), it wasn't a traditional Irish step that I had ever encountered and it was danced very differently in terms of style. This is an example of a step that is used to demonstrate the Irish component of the island's cultural identity. Even with similar gestural motifs, the heel and toe takes on a completely different meaning in the Montserratian context. What I ultimately came away with was how enticing these "exotic" narratives of Irish and African cultural encounters are, as though they are two sides of a very stark binary. The reality, of course, is much more complex, and I learned that Montserratians have very complicated feelings about how much these identities are played up, depending on how connected they may feel to Irish or African heritage. And all of this can be triggered by conversations about just one step, the heel and toe polka. This research is why I am concerned about attributing Africanist aesthetics to "White" forms like *sean nós*. I see it as a rebranding of the tradition to show how it has also been marginalized—a sort of "Me-Too-ism" in dance. I have seen a lot of problematic debates about, for example, whether Irish indentured servants in the Americas were treated as badly as enslaved Africans.[8] It is so interesting how the stories we tell about the meaning of our steps and styles develop along with the narratives we construct about our own identities.

Sinclair: In my experience, Black people often talk about the erasure of our identities and contributions, and about not being seen in general. This includes when we complain about how what is being done to us affects us mentally, emotionally, and physically. Along that line of thought, I often say that the system of colonization, racism, and erasure affects everyone, including Westerners and White people. In dance specifically, anything outside of what is valued in the mainstream is at risk of being erased for not being legitimate, legible, or valuable. It is no wonder that many people are now seeing that they are somehow affected by these inequities and that their voices are not being heard. Not everyone has experienced the same level of marginalization, but many people across the globe have been affected simultaneously. However, I have noticed that when a group of people faces marginalization, they turn to others who have been marginalized for guidance or inspiration on how to navigate the experience. This is true for many African nations, as they have constantly sought the insight of other nations for help navigating such complexities. At times they have ended up teaming up against forces they deem oppressive. For example, African leaders looked to African American leaders during the Civil Rights Movement to initiate a similar freedom fight referred to as Pan-Africanism in the 1950s and 1960s. In relation to dance origins, I always try to remember what history is and who curates that history. Do we have this history about Irish dance and any African dance coming into contact documented, and, if so, who is promoting this history and whom does it serve? Without knowing, we cannot objectively answer most of these complex questions. I see why the simplistic narrative that all these percussive dances came from Africanist practices can be problematic. But what if improvisational and percussive dances *were* invented by Africans? What would be so wrong with that? I am curious about what this could mean.

Kate: I don't think there would be anything wrong with it. But I am uncomfortable with continuing to rely on a binary that pits "White against Black" and "Europeanist against Africanist" when the reality is that White and Black, or European and African, cultural forms have often intermingled, especially in the Americas. Our conversation here has been about calling attention to the fact that there has been a prejudice against anything improvisational as "non-intellectual," and we see that prejudice, to varying degrees, across racial lines. I think only looking at race ignores some of the complexities related to intellectualism and elitism in both art and academia, which also touch on ethnicity and class, among other variables. I am concerned that binary thinking is preventing us from doing more nuanced dance studies work that reflects these confluences. Even just the two of us having this dialogue about how we perceive and value our own forms as we have navigated different spaces throughout the world demonstrates how complex this topic is.

Sinclair: I agree with you here. This is why in Chapter 5 we dive deeper into what it means to document such steps and construct archives and historical narratives in dance. We are not just complaining. We have a vision for how we can responsibly delve into these histories. This work is about producing archives of embodied knowledge that can help alleviate the issues with such binary thinking in order to advance our community dances, methodologies, and creative and intellectual works. For both of us, the next step after deeply examining our steps, whether choreographed or improvised, is to think about how we remember them, pass them on, and recognize the knowledge they produce.

***

In summary, our framework for cultural confluences requires us to think through intellectualism and elitism in dance based on the idea that the cultural codes found in some dance forms are meaningful, while others are "just steps." In particular, we point to prejudices around the ways that dances are produced, through choreography and improvisation, and how each has been and continues to be racialized as White and Black systems of dance creation, respectively. While these categories may describe each system in general, they are not adequate for describing the nuances of different forms. We are interested in how this division came to be and how Western ideologies about aesthetic value perpetuate this separation. To show the complexity of these issues beyond Black/White and African/European binaries, we question what the common denominator is between forms that have been reduced to "just steps" across racial, ethnic, or cultural lines. That is, we are interested in what happens in confluent spaces where dancers have intermingled and continue to do so, making it difficult to fully attribute influences to one primary source.

Steps, tradition, and contemporaneity

The question of how to participate in our academic and professional dance fields often boils down to what it means to contribute to the field. In our own ways, both of us are concerned with how to be relevant and not simply perform steps but communicate something meaningful and multi-layered as contemporary artists and scholars. Here we use the word "contemporary" broadly, as dancers who are creating work today. We believe that what is considered contemporary in dance does not mean adopting mainstream Western aesthetics and approaches to creating dance. What is contemporary can and should arise from the practitioner and whatever movement background they come from, not just one mainstream dance culture.

The interlude that follows serves as a segue into our final chapter. In it, Kate describes Irish dance artist Colin Dunne's "Concert" (2019), a contemporary piece that works within the Irish dance tradition by calling steps, tunes, and historical archives into the performance space through embodied percussive sounding, sets, and projection design. The work exemplifies how meaning is created and conveyed in a contemporary setting that nods, and also "tilts," the head toward tradition. The interlude illustrates various ideas from this chapter about how steps are made meaningful, as Dunne interfaces with tradition in ways that can be appreciated by outsiders but also riffs on particular codes in steps and rhythms that are meaningful to insiders. In addition, Dunne uses improvisational methods to work with tunes that would normally be accompanied by traditionally choreographed steps, suggesting the possibility for playfulness and spontaneity that may have been largely written out of mainstream traditional Irish dance over the past 100 years.

***

Interlude by Kate: When steps echo meaning

In November 2019, I took the bus from Washington, D.C., up to New York City to see Irish dancer and choreographer Colin Dunne's solo show called "Concert." "Concert" was Dunne's interpretation of Tommie Potts' 1972 solo fiddle album, *The Liffey Banks*, which is infamous in traditional Irish music for its idiosyncrasies, its contradictions, and for being completely "undanceable." On the album, Potts plays his reels, jigs, hornpipes, and slip jigs with starts and stops, stutters, contractions and expansions, and sudden changes in tempo. Potts passed away in 1988, having released just this one album, and Dunne wanted to engage with it so that audiences could see—and more importantly, hear—Irish traditional music and dance in a new way.

I listened to *The Liffey Banks* for the first time on the bus ride to New York and I found it both intriguing and uncomfortable. As competitive Irish dancers, we are trained to dance within the "grid" of the musical structure, which, at competitions, is governed by a steady metronome. Listening to Potts' fiddle, I felt my stomach literally drop at each unexpected turn, but I was also delighted by the way he made me "tilt" my head, to borrow the word that Dunne used in an interview with dancer Edwina Guckian (2021). I was most uncomfortable listening to "The Blackbird," which is a well-known Irish set dance, a piece of choreography that is set to a specific tune and is part of the traditional repertoire that Irish step dancers learn early on in their training. The purpose of such "sounded" dances is not just to dance to the music, but to make music by "dancing the tune" (Gareiss 2011). When I hear a familiar tune like "The Blackbird," I immediately begin to hear the dance's counterpoint rhythm in my head, but, in Potts' rendition, I could only hook into a handful of short phrases or runs.

In "Concert," Dunne and his team, directed by Sinéad Rushe, utilized different sound technologies to dismantle the centrality of the visual aspects of Irish dance, locating the meaning of Irish dance cultural knowledge instead in the sounds of steps and tunes. The stage at New York's Baryshnikov Arts Center was equipped with three plywood dance floors (ideal for hard shoe sounding), and the set included a record player with a vinyl copy of Potts' *Liffey Banks*, a piano, a fiddle, a pair of dance shoes, and a cassette recorder. Through sound design by Mel Mercier and lighting design by Colin Grenfell, Dunne "called" tradition into the space through projections and recordings of decades-old archival footage from Irish dance and music history. From speakers placed around the room, we heard Potts' fiddle playing and his voice coming from various locations at different volumes, rather than piped through the central sound system, giving an even stronger impression that he was in the room with us. While the music itself, as I listened to it on the bus ride, had already made me "tilt" my head in curiosity, this effect in the space made me physically lean toward the sound, as though getting closer to it would make it more comprehensible.

One of the most powerful segments in the hour-long concert was Dunne's contrived conversation with a disembodied Potts, whom he brought back to life through sound alone, through a small speaker placed upstage right. In the segment, Dunne sits on a chair to strap on his shoes, and we hear sound bites from an old archival interview with Potts. Dunne begins a bantering, playful, and very funny conversation with the fiddler, whose voice is raspy and scratchy due to the quality of the old recording. Potts urges Dunne to hurry up and start dancing, to which Dunne responds, exasperated, "Hold on just two seconds, let me get my shoes on!" Potts starts playing. "Oh, okay, you're not going to wait? Here we go then." At the end of the piece, Dunne sits down again, breathless, as Potts comments with a touch of reluctance in his voice, "That was quite good," and Dunne, in a somewhat defeated tone, responds, "Yeah, that wasn't too bad?"

Later came "The Blackbird," the unsettling set dance tune that I had listened to on the bus. Although set dances are not improvised, they trace the melodic structure with footwork. Set dances are set to a particular melody—not just any piece of music in a given time signature like a reel or a jig—and the percussive sound is meant to echo the melody. "The Blackbird" itself is already a "crooked" tune, with just 7.5 bars instead of the standard 8, but I couldn't even count bars in Potts' version. Dunne sat down at the piano and first played an upbeat, vamping version of the tune as we commonly know it. He spoke briefly about "The Blackbird" as a traditional set dance and tune, and then he awkwardly echoed short phrases from Potts' recording on the keys. Again, as on the bus, I felt my body yearning to latch onto familiar phrasings, my feet activated and twitching in my seat, but it was just too "crooked," too "tilted." I waited anxiously for Dunne, one of the greatest rhythmic Irish dancers of our time, to get up and dance it.

He didn't.

I was astonished and was almost brought to tears by the silence—his respectful admission that he could not dance it or, perhaps, that he refused to. It meant so much to me, as an audience member well entrenched in the tradition, to not hear something in the space, but to *feel* the echoes of my corporeal knowledge vibrate through my Irish dancing body. I felt the archive that lives within me become activated in those few short minutes. The experience made me realize how much is in there, waiting to be interpellated.

Besides this silence in "The Blackbird," I was delighted by Dunne's playfulness throughout the concert, which was created through an improvisational process. Improvisation is rare in competitive Irish step dance today, whereas it is more common in other percussive forms like tap, flamenco, flatfooting, and *sean nós* and other older Irish dance styles. In a review, arts writer Eva Yaa Asantewaa noted, "It was impossible to be a tap dance fan and not sit there mentally pairing him with tap artists—Black ones in particular—soul to soul" (2019). I was interested in this comparison because of its implicit reference to the complicated history of aligning transatlantic Blackness and Irish cultural identity. I wondered what prompted her to pair him with Black tap artists. His rhythm? His playful improvisation? The looseness in his arms and upper body? In Dunne's conversation with Potts, both men showed how intentional instability, resistance to reductive categories, improvisation, and a certain playfulness or "tilting of the head" also play a role in Irish music and dance.

I am not sure to what extent Dunne might have been influenced by Africanist aesthetics and Black improvisational methodologies, whether through his contemporary dance training, his collaborations with tap dancers, or other influences. But I also think about how much of this improvisational, playful quality already is and always has been a part of Irish dance. Dunne implemented choreographic methodologies outside of today's mainstream Irish dance tradition, specifically by embodying Potts' notoriously undanceable sound and bringing it into the present day. In this way, he demonstrated how Irish dancers can engage with "just steps" to reconstruct an embodied archive through what we hear, and perhaps more importantly, what we don't hear.

***

Conclusion

This chapter has examined the value of steps in traditional dance forms and the central role they play in creating meaning for a community. We have questioned the role of intellectualization and abstraction in modern and postmodern dance and how these processes become complicated for dance forms that are culturally and racially marked in mainstream Western spaces. As a point of entry to explore the ownership or origin of particular steps and movement practices in one or another culture, we turned to our experiences as practitioners of Nigerian and Irish dance forms in the United States to unpack the specific dynamics of African and Irish cultural encounters in the Americas.

The final interlude about Colin Dunne's creative work in Irish dance provides one example of how steps can frame one's relationship to tradition, on the one hand, and contemporaneity, on the other. In the following chapter, we build on this theme in the realm of academic scholarship in dance, considering how we can develop archival and ethnographic research methods that better encapsulate the instability of historical interpretation in confluent dance spaces. We consider what it means to archive the dance, or dance the archive, to promote cultural knowledge production within communities.

Notes

1 Kate expands on the idea of steps and stories in her essay, "Irish Dance on Repeat: Archiving the Dance and Dancing the Archive," commissioned for Jean Butler's "Our Steps" dialogue series; see https://www.our-steps.com/dialogue/irish-dance-on-repeat-archiving-the-dance-and-dancing-the-archive (Spanos 2022).
2 Kate was a student in the Master's in Traditional Irish Dance Performance program at the University of Limerick from 2007–2008, under the directorship of Dr. Catherine Foley. For more about the design and development of the Master's program, which Foley launched in 1999, see her articles, "The Roots and Routes of Irish Step Dancing: Issues of Identity and Participation in a Global World" (2012b) and "Contesting and Negotiating Hegemonic Discourses: Constructing and Developing a Master's Programme in Irish Traditional Dance Performance within a University Context" (2021).
3 As described in *The Individual and Tradition* edited by Cashman, Mould, and Shukla, tradition can be conceptualized as a static resource or a dynamic process. The latter definition suggests a more active approach to tradition as recycling, transfer, transformation, and circulation. The individual in a tradition has agency while also working as part of a collectivity. This conceptualization suggests the dynamic nature of tradition, which is difficult to pin down in the ways that Western capitalist culture demands (2011, 1–26).
4 Choreographer Miguel Gutierrez asks, "Does Abstraction Belong to White People?" in his 2018 essay about racial identity in modern and contemporary dance. The essay points to the ways that racial identity in American contemporary dance determines whose work needs "interpretation" and whose work can remain "abstract."
5 The term "anti-structure" refers to anthropologist Victor Turner's study of the structure and anti-structure of ritual (1969) and carnival (1986), as well as Brazilian anthropologist Roberto Da Matta's conceptualization of carnival in various structural planes and social domains (1984, 1991).
6 For more about dance master Nascimento do Passo and the process of frevo's "spectacularization," "professionalization," and "academicization," see work of Maria Goretti Rocha de Oliveira (1993, 2017) and Valéria Vicente (2009).
7 For perspectives on the racialization of the Irish in Ireland and the United States, see Noel Ignatiev's *How the Irish Became White* (1995) and Steven Garner's *Racism in the Irish Experience* (2004) and "How the Irish Became White (Again)" (2007). The following authors have written about Irish/Scots Irish and African encounters in the context of culture, music, and dance, including the history of Irish performers in blackface minstrelsy: Lott (1993), Nowatzki (2006), O'Neill and Lloyd (2009), Hill (2010), Onkey (2010), Greaves (2012), and Jamison (2015).
8 For some examples of writings about Irish or White slaves in the Americas, see Akenson (1997), O'Callaghan (2001), and Jordan and Walsh (2008).

References

Akenson, Donald Harman. 1997. *If the Irish Ran the World: Montserrat, 1630–1730*. Montreal, Quebéc: McGill-Queen's University Press.
Asantewaa, Eva Yaa. 2019. "Stepping out: Colin Dunne's 'Concert' at BAC." *InfiniteBody* (blog). https://infinitebody.blogspot.com/2019/11/stepping-out-colin-dunnes-concert-at-bac.html.

Bannerman, Henrietta. 2014. "Is Dance a Language? Movement, Meaning and Communication." *Dance Research: The Journal of the Society for Dance Research* 32 (1): 65–80.

Bastos, Otávio, dir. 2018. *Qual a relação entre o frevo e a capoeira?* Mexe Com Tudo. https://www.youtube.com/watch?v=0SDvuNJRaaU.

Brennan, Helen. 2001. *The Story of Irish Dance*. Lanham, MD: Roberts Rinehart Publishers.

Buckland, Theresa. 1983. "Definitions of Folk Dance: Some Explorations." *Folk Music Journal* 4 (4): 315–32.

Cashman, Ray, Tom Mould, and Pravina Shukla. 2011. *The Individual and Tradition: Folkloristic Perspectives*. Special Publications of the Folklore Institute 8. Bloomington, IN: Indiana University Press.

Chaleff, Rebecca. 2018. "Activating Whiteness: Racializing the Ordinary in US American Postmodern Dance." *Dance Research Journal* 50 (3): 71–84. https://doi.org/10.1017/S0149767718000372.

Cullinane, John. 1987. *Aspects of the History of Irish Dancing in Ireland, England, New Zealand, North America and Australia*. Cork City: Dr. John P. Cullinane.

Da Matta, Roberto. 1984. "Carnival in Multiple Planes." In *Rite, Drama, Festival, Spectacle: Rehearsals Toward a Critical Performance*, edited by John J. MacAloon, 208–39. Philadelphia, PA: Institute for the Study of Human Issues.

———. 1991. *Carnivals, Rogues, and Heroes: An Interpretation of the Brazilian Dilemma*. Notre Dame, IN: University of Notre Dame Press.

de Oliveira, Valdemar. 1985. *Frevo, capoeira e "passo."* 2nd edition. Recife: Companhia Editora de Pernambuco.

Dixon-Gottschild, Brenda. 1998. *Digging the Africanist Presence in American Performance: Dance and Other Contexts*. Westport, CT: Praeger Publishers.

Dunne, Colin. 2022. "Summer Reading: Colin Dunne." *Our Steps: Recording, Reflecting & Reimaging Irish Dance* (blog). https://www.our-steps.com/dialogue/summer-reading-colin-dunne.

Emoghene, Sinclair Ogaga. 2007. "Nigerian Contemporary Dance Creation: Human Emotion and Passion as the Basis for Dance Choreography." Benin City, Edo State, Nigeria: University of Benin.

Foley, Catherine E. 2001. "Perceptions of Irish Step Dance: National, Global, and Local." *Dance Research Journal* 33: 34–45.

———. 2011. "The Irish Céilí: A Site for Constructing, Experiencing, and Negotiating a Sense of Community and Identity." *Dance Research: The Journal of the Society for Dance Research* 29 (1): 43–60.

———. 2012a. "Ethnochoreology as a Mediating Perspective in Irish Dance Studies." *New Hibernia Review* 16 (2): 143–54. https://doi.org/10.1353/nhr.2012.0024.

———. 2012b. "The Roots and Routes of Irish Step Dancing: Issues of Identity and Participation in a Global World." *Routes and Roots: Fiddle and Dance Studies from around the North Atlantic 4*, 145–56.

———. 2013. *Step Dancing in Ireland: Culture and History*. Burlington, VT: Ashgate.

———. 2021. "Contesting and Negotiating Hegemonic Discourses: Constructing and Developing a Master's Programme in Irish Traditional Dance Performance within a University Context." In *The Artist and Academia*, edited by Helen Phelan and Graham F. Welch, 181–201. London, UK: Routledge.

Gareiss, Nic. 2011. "Dance the Tune: A Listening-Based Approach to Percussive Step Dance." In *2011 Congress on Research in Dance Joint Conference with the Society of Ethnomusicology.*

Garner, Steven. 2004. *Racism in the Irish Experience*. London, UK: Pluto Press.

———. 2007. "How the Irish Became White (Again)." In *Whiteness: An Introduction*, 120–35. London, UK: Routledge.

Goretti Rocha de Oliveira, Maria. 1993. *Danças populares como espetáculo público no Recife de 1970 a 1988*. Recife: Fundação do Patrimônio Histórico e Artístico de Pernambuco/Secretaria de Educação, Cultura e Esportes.

———. 2017. *Frevo: A Choreological Performance*. Recife: Richard Veiga.

Greaves, Margaret. 2012. "Slave Ships and Coffin Ships: Transatlantic Exchanges in Irish-American Blackface Minstrelsy." *Comparative American Studies* 10: 78–94.

Guckian, Edwina, dir. 2021. Dance on The Box Day 4. Leitrim Dance Festival.

Gutierrez, Miguel. 2018. "Does Abstraction Belong to White People?" *BOMB Magazine*, November 7, 2018. https://bombmagazine.org/articles/miguel-gutierrez-1/.

Hill, Constance Valis. 2010. *Tap Dancing America: A Cultural History*. Oxford, UK: Oxford University Press.

Hobsbawm, Eric, and Terence Ranger. 1983. *The Invention of Tradition*. Cambridge, UK: Cambridge University Press.

Ignatiev, Noel. 1995. *How the Irish Became White*. New York, NY: Routledge.

Jamison, Phil. 2015. *Hoedowns, Reels, and Frolics: Roots and Branches of Southern Appalachian Dance*. Music in American Life. Urbana, IL: University of Illinois Press.

Jordan, Don, and Michael Walsh. 2008. *White Cargo: The Forgotten History of Britain's White Slaves in America*. New York, NY: New York University Press.

Kealiinohomoku, Joann Wheeler. 1972. "Folk Dance." In *Folklore & Folklife: An Introduction*, edited by Richard M. Dorson. Chicago, IL: University of Chicago Press.

———. 1983. "An Anthropologist Looks at Ballet as a Form of Ethnic Dance." In *What Is Dance?: Readings in Theory and Criticism*, edited by Roger Copeland and Marshall Cohen, 33–43. Oxford, UK: Oxford University Press.

Lott, Eric. 1993. *Love and Theft: Blackface Minstrelsy and the American Working Class*. Oxford, UK: Oxford University Press.

Manning, Susan. 2004. *Modern Dance, Negro Dance: Race in Motion*. Minneapolis, MN: University of Minnesota Press.

Nahachewsky, Andriy. 2001. "Once Again: On the Concept of 'Second Existence Folk Dance.'" *Yearbook for Traditional Music* 33: 17–28.

Nowatzki, Robert. 2006. "Paddy Jumps Jim Crow: Irish-Americans and Blackface Minstrelsy." *Éire-Ireland* 41: 162–84.

O'Callaghan, Sean. 2001. *To Hell or Barbados: The Ethnic Cleansing of Ireland*. London, UK: Brandon.

O'Neill, Peter D., and David Lloyd. 2009. *The Black and Green Atlantic: Cross-Currents of the African and Irish Diasporas*. London, UK: Palgrave Macmillan.

Onkey, Lauren. 2010. *Blackness and Transatlantic Irish Identity: Celtic Soul Brothers*. New York, NY: Routledge.

Spanos, Kathleen A. 2017. "Dancing the Archive: Rhythms of Change in Montserrat's Masquerades." *Yearbook for Traditional Music* 49: 67–91. https://doi.org/10.5921/yeartradmusi.49.2017.0067.

———. 2019a. "A Dance of Resistance from Recife, Brazil: Carnivalesque Improvisation in Frevo." *Dance Research Journal* 51 (3): 28–46. https://doi.org/10.1017/S0149767719000305.

———. 2019b. "Locating Montserrat Between the Black and Green." *Irish Migration Studies in Latin America* 9 (2): 1–14.

————. 2022. "Irish Dance on Repeat: Archiving the Dance and Dancing the Archive." *Our Steps: Recording, Reflecting & Reimaging Irish Dance* (blog). https://www.our-steps.com/dialogue/irish-dance-on-repeat-archiving-the-dance-and-dancing-the-archive.

Turner, Victor. 1969. *The Ritual Process: Structure and Anti-Structure*. The Lewis Henry Morgan Lectures, 1966. Chicago, IL: Aldine Publishing Company.

————. 1986. "Carnival in Rio: Dionysian Drama in an Industrializing Society." In *The Anthropology of Performance*, 103–24. New York, NY: PAJ Publications.

Vicente, Ana Valéria. 2009. *Entre a ponta de pé e o calcanhar: reflexões sobre como o frevo encena o povo, a nação e a dança no Recife*. Recife: Editora Universitária da UFPE.

5 Cultural knowledge production in dance academia

Throughout this book, we have asked if we actually belong in mainstream academic spaces, or if academia is not the place for us as artists and scholars of non-mainstream dance forms. We have questioned why we stay in these spaces if we feel that our work is not valued or understood. We have considered whether we need to engage in this struggle or stay within our communities where we have more freedom to dance on our own terms. Throughout the process of writing and dialoguing with each other about these questions, we have concluded that we do, in fact, belong. We have determined that there are ways to accommodate and include dancers from non-mainstream forms in academic and professional spaces by changing the language that is used to talk about dance; reassessing our approaches to aesthetic evaluation and spatial configuration; and reevaluating how we think about creative processes in dance. This chapter offers ideas about what will help us advocate for ourselves, as young researchers, to contribute the value that we know we bring to the field. We belong in these spaces. And in this chapter, we articulate how we could be better supported as part of a more diverse, equitable, and inclusive environment.

The preceding chapter's concluding interlude about Colin Dunne's contemporary Irish dance performance exemplified working within a traditional form in innovative ways, calling in archival voices and sounds from that tradition in ways that playfully demonstrate the instability of historical authority. We now ask how we can better communicate culturally specific values in dance academia, which is itself a confluent space made up of artists and scholars from various dance forms, some of which are more mainstream and better supported than others. As we have argued throughout this book, the broad categories that are currently used to describe dance genres, such as "African dance" or "world dance," hinder the study and practice of cultural specificity in our field. By relying on established frameworks in Western academia, cultures within these broad categories that have already been widely studied continue to gain more visibility in the literature, and they, in turn, become established as dominant cultures relative to others.

As we describe throughout this chapter, we are specifically concerned with the fact that the cultural knowledge we bring to the field as dancers from non-mainstream forms is channeled into mainstream education and used to further promote Western studies. By participating in (and being paid by) Western academic

DOI: 10.4324/9781003231226-6

institutions, both of us pull from our communities of study, but we do not necessarily have the resources to also give back. That is, what we contribute to dance in academia (including the publication of this book) goes into a Western knowledge bank and is evaluated as a Western work, whether or not it is about Western dance. Our work does not make it back to the communities we aim to serve without intentional efforts to do so.

Whereas other chapters focused on the creation and performance of dance, this chapter is specifically about dance scholarship, including the use of archival and ethnographic research methods in our field. We envision what records and sources about dances from around the world could look like within our framework of cultural confluences and networks of migratory dance communities. Whereas this book has so far focused primarily on points of spatial confluence for artists migrating across different cultures throughout the world, here we add the dimension of time and generational transmission. The notion of archival documentation often calls to mind images of the archaic and ancient, but archives can also provide a vision of what we might be able to accomplish in the future. As Jacques Derrida writes, "The question of the archive is not … a question of the past. It is a question of the future … of a responsibility for tomorrow. The archive: if we want to know what this will have meant, we will only know in the times to come" (1996, 27). Dance is a physical art-making process in which movements are absorbed by the body at a particular moment in time, but the dance experience is also elongated in that individual dancing bodies arise from their pasts and continue to breathe into the future. Just as we attempted in previous chapters to complicate the notion of rigid categories or boundaries for defining dance forms and practitioners, we also consider how a chronological sense of time does not fully describe how dancers relate to their dance culture's history and even their personal histories within that dance form. And yet, this is often the approach that is taken in academic scholarship, especially with regard to the traditional dance cultures that both of us practice.

In the archiving of cultural objects, artifacts and documents are physically housed in a place like a library, museum, or other institutional center designed to accumulate knowledge. Information scientist Robin Boast argues that, contrary to James Clifford's idea that a museum is a contact zone where reciprocal transcultural encounters take place (1997), it is actually a site of asymmetrical power that serves the neocolonial center where "leftover colonial competences—collecting, exhibiting, and educating" take place and where cultural knowledge is "constantly generalize[d], constantly summarize[d], constantly standardize[d]" (2011, 65). Boast argues that museums should cede control of resources, artifacts, and objects to communities to support greater collaboration and sharing of authority with respect to cultural information. We see dancers as uniquely positioned to take on this kind of work since a dance first lives in the body itself—the individual body and the collective body.

We also draw on methods in critical ethnography (Madison 2020) to support not only listening to communities and reflecting their own language and concepts in our research but also to provide agency for them to contribute to the documentation of their dance practices. We seek approaches that will help us create more flexible, community-centered, and community-built frameworks for the documentation of cultural knowledge—approaches that do not require the use of limiting and dichotomous categories, colonialist language, or chronological timelines. Such documentation will help us organize and catalog information in ways that are meaningful to communities, not just to academics. For example, some records of African dance forms housed at the Library of Congress are filed under offensive, colonialist terms such as "bushmen," rather than sorted by actual ethnic groups, types of dances, or other helpful keywords that locals would use to describe themselves. There is no way for a researcher looking for information about, for example, the *Inu-Ani* dance of Nigeria to find those keywords in the library's online catalog. We are also interested in taking an approach to dance scholarship about non-mainstream forms that leans into complexity and leaves room for conflict, change, and disagreement about such terminology within the archive itself—an approach that is process-oriented, rather than product-oriented, to better represent how meaning develops over time in dance communities.

We have seen how archival records can be used to define and justify territorial lines in ways that divide, exclude, and marginalize. From the need for representation in academic scholarship emerges the fraught demand that we express ownership over our dance cultures, which involves some policing of authenticity and claiming of territory. Limited funding and resources force this ideology in many ways, and this limitation is prevalent in confluent spaces where multiple groups co-exist, deepening the divisions between mainstream and non-mainstream categories. Considerations of ownership often boil down to royalties, which are rare in traditional, folk, and other community-based dance forms because there is often less value placed on how dance is sold or exchanged. As we noted in Chapter 1, Susan Leigh Foster describes two spheres of exchange in dance: the commodity and the gift. She argues that dance is valuable in the global marketplace because it is always transactional: it is either sold as a product, exchanged for physical and emotional "energy," or used to build relationships (2019). We question whether we are locked into our current capitalist framework for research, which always values dance as transactional, or whether there are technologies and research techniques that would allow us to break out of this structure and support communities in ways that promote the sharing of dance energies as a goal unto itself. As we have stated throughout this book, defining what is traditional or authentic in a dance culture is important for representation, but it can also hinder the development of the form when taken to the extreme. In practice, the borders that define a dance form are never clear and often debated, even (or perhaps more so) in ostensibly rigid forms. In this chapter, we propose looking to dance communities to build more inclusive archival processes so that they maintain ownership and control over how their cultural knowledge is accessed and used.

For us, giving back to dance communities is not only about financial or economic contributions but also involves: (1) promoting local methodologies in academic research; (2) developing traceable footprints that tie cultural practices to communities; and (3) creating open access to information within communities through indigenous communication methods and links between large worldwide institutions and smaller local institutions. We propose building on traditional archival and ethnographic methods for documenting dance creation, presentation, transmission, and reconstruction ("Documenting Dance" 2006) by considering dance origins, dwellings, and usages through the archeo-historiographical methods of provenance (where an object originated), provenience (where an object was found), and context (how an object is interpreted within its cultural milieu) (Flexner 2016). Sinclair first hit upon these methods in 2020 while initiating his "Living Archive" research project, which aims to create an interactive map-based platform that details the origins and migrations of African and African diasporic dance forms through data visualization and collation (described in more detail later in this chapter). Having successfully developed modalities that can show and simulate relationships formed through translation, transmission, and retention of African dance cultures with shared trajectories, it was important to him to also find a way for communities to use and benefit from what he envisions to be a hub of cultural knowledge capital. In talking with museum scientists, he was drawn to provenance, provenience, and context to describe where dances are found, who dances them, how transmission continues, and how dances shape experience and identity through migrations over time.

Provenance, provenience, and context provide a framework for us to consider the life cycles and adaptation of different dance cultures within confluent spaces, expanding on traditional archiving methods by providing community access to archives, creating a two-way feedback system rather than the simple storage of information. It is not enough to merely invite communities to collect their history using methodologies formulated by Western scholarship. Unlike treating an archive as an end goal in and of itself, we advocate for a process that invites community members to bring their own knowledge to the table, identify their own origins, and retain their cultural history within the community through indigenous practices. In this way, communities would be given visibility and agency to document their dance cultures in their own ways without being mediated by Western scholarship. In short, the approach we are proposing is about allowing people to use the methods that already exist in their communities for their own benefit in the realm of academic research.

Thus, this final chapter draws on our examinations of language, aesthetics, space, and dance-making in previous chapters to propose approaches to academic dance research within our framework of cultural confluences. There is—and has long been—a critical need to reframe dance traditions in ways that encompass the full nature and function of dance forms in their specific contexts. We call for reconsideration and expansion of what makes a "scholar" or "historian" in dance studies, especially in studies of non-mainstream dance forms that have been underrepresented in academia. We begin by examining current archival processes in dance. Then we outline how provenance, provenience, and context can be used for conducting archival research on dance cultures to be more inclusive of communities of origin, taking into account both local communication practices and technological solutions in our work.

Dancing the archive, archiving the dance

In academia, the quintessential marker of "real history" is written text, and we, as scholars, are compelled to seek, find, and interpret the facts left behind by previous generations. Without a history documented in writing, a dance culture may be seen as less legitimate or valuable in academic circles. To archive something often gives it a timestamp of reference, marking the beginning of something's history, which can cancel out the contributions, additions, and outgrowths that have branched off from a dance's known and documented origin. We believe that the idea that dance can be presented as an archivable object ultimately inhibits a deeper understanding of how dance practices continually develop across bodies and generations in confluent environments. We are concerned that academic study of such cultures leaves living people behind in favor of citing objects as historical evidence, forgetting that knowledge about how an object is used, made, or danced is often more important than preserving that object's materiality and its so-called authenticity. For example, Sinclair notes that, in Nigeria, an artifact like a mask from the distant past is valued more for its historical and artistic worth than masks made today by those who continue such mask-making practices. Today's practitioners, then, become secondary to the historical artifact itself. To counter this sort of obsession with the past, historian Chris Ballard takes a perspective on historicity as "privileg[ing] the performative and the sensory" to consider how history is performed and perceived, especially in the present day and through mutual influences in the process of cultural encounters (2014, 107–111). We see dance studies as particularly suited to expand on archival methodologies so that they reflect the nature of embodied culture as ever-changing, migratory, and organic in the most literal sense of the word.

The word "archive" often invokes images of databases, historical artifacts, and dusty paperwork stored in a library, representing the endurance and survival of material culture that benefits Western knowledge production by a single author or creator. As archivist Jennifer Douglas states, "The concept of creatorship is central to archival theory. Archives are acquired because of who creates them ...." (2018, 30). According to standards of archival description, an archival creator is a person or entity that "created, accumulated, and/or maintained records," not to be confused with the "collector" (qtd. in Douglas 2018, 30). She points out that archivists are generally trained to emphasize the perspective of a single creator and not implement methods that fully take into account the role of community in archival creation. Individual researchers become the published "creators" of an archive, retaining copyright over their written work and intellectual property.

Dance forms, like other intangible cultural practices, have been "salvaged" at major archival institutions, preserved in Western frameworks that enforce a logical and scientific, but ultimately fixed, structure of understanding based on a single perspective. Sinclair notes that foreign scholarship methods have been so prevalent in studies of dance cultures from his own country, especially during Nigeria's postcolonial era, that younger researchers now depend on these studies as the main sources of information about their own culture (e.g., Chernoff 1979; Enekwe 1991;

Ajayi-Soyinka 1998; Gore 1999). Such scholarship contributes greatly to the field, but we also believe that the prevalence of Western methods in African dance studies perpetuates the idea that only academics working within a Western framework can contribute to a dance culture's archival records. Even with advances in academic fields toward more equity and better representation of African and African diasporic dances, much of this scholarship has not been revisited, reinterpreted, or reimagined by people from these communities.

Sinclair has also noticed how, in more recent years, African dance methods have taken root in the wider turn toward somatic-centered, practice-based research in the academy (Barrett and Bolt 2007; Smith and Dean 2009; Phelan and Welch 2021). This is a positive step, but he notes that histories of African dance forms that are less known and not represented in the mainstream global African dance category (such as his Urhobo dances) are largely missing in academic literature, despite the large amount of information that lives in corporeal and cultural memory within these communities. There is relatively little modern documentation in texts and films of these lesser-known forms, and what does exist is often incorrect and based on ill-informed outsider interpretations. The lack of documentation over decades makes African dance history appear simplistic in the archive, but it is, of course, as complex as any other dance history. Stronger historical accounts would allow scholars and artists of these forms to compete for research development, funding resources, training opportunities, and preservation resources. Improved processes for documenting dance cultures and their histories would also enable local artists and scholars to establish ownership and gain remuneration and reparation amidst the challenges of globalization, cultural appropriation, and the constantly changing terrain of "culture."

In light of the challenges around the documentation of dance forms that are underrepresented in the archive, we question whether "archive" is even the proper term to use and whether or not it is actually possible to archive dance, on the one hand, or dance an archive, on the other. What exactly are we archiving when we archive dance? We think about dance as archive in two ways: (1) dance as the actual embodiment of cultural knowledge that is transmitted and transposed from physical body to physical body; and (2) dance as a figurative receptacle that holds memories and perpetuates historical narratives that promote cultural identity formation. The former perspective considers the body itself as an archive, focusing on the technical and physical components of the dance, as well as details about how the body itself moves. For example, as a traditional Irish dancer, Kate senses that she carries an archive of steps in her body. She feels that she carries neural patterns, collected[1] and encoded in her physical body, that represent the specificity of the tradition she participates in. Sinclair, however, feels that it is impossible for him to carry an archive in his body alone because he is constantly negotiating the usefulness of different elements of his embodied knowledge. For him, the process of embodying elements of a dance contributes to a repository of memories that then become available for future recall and use. Being in a group of people also supports memory by seeing others do the "right" movements and falling into step with them. So, for him, it is not just about one individual body carrying an archive alone.

Sinclair feels that those who do think of their bodies as an archive, like Kate, are responding to pressures to "own" a cultural practice that is threatened or seen as illegitimate, which he believes is not an ideal motivation for storing cultural information in the body. The two of us have considered that our different perspectives on this arise from the differences between how cultural information is carried in newly migrated bodies (like Sinclair's, from Nigeria to the United States) as compared to bodies that have not migrated geographically (like Kate's, growing up in the Irish American diaspora). These differences are reflected in our dialogues in the previous chapter about how we think about our "steps" in the context of choreography and collecting versus improvisation and strategic negotiation. Sinclair's dancing while growing up in Nigeria was embedded in his everyday life, whereas Kate's was a hobby, existing separately from what was expected of her in everyday life in the United States, a confluent space with many cultural forms vying for attention. Being an Irish dancer from the United States has felt to her like being a collector of steps, absorbing cultural knowledge about her Irish heritage that otherwise felt quite distant. Thus, the ways we migrate and come into contact with cultural differences determine how we hold, perceive, and display this information in our bodies.

One concern we have with the perspective of dance as a physical archive is the assumption that such knowledge always remains unchanged, or that there is a pure version of the dance out there that exists that bodies strive to attain and maintain in physical practice. With traditional Irish dance steps, Kate senses that archival material is passed down through dances that do not and should not change. For example, to be considered "authentic," a traditional dancer should mimic one's teacher technically and stylistically. However, even in forms like Irish step dance in which imitation is an integral part of maintaining tradition and authenticity, no two bodies dance a step exactly the same way, not only due to age or body type but also because of one's stylistic training and sense of musicality. After generations of passing down steps, we will never know what the original looked like, so is this really an archive of the past? If the archive is perceived as being about continuity and precise imitation over time, then we lose the specificity of individuals who contributed to that archive, each of whom plays a crucial role in developing the form. A system of archiving that is built to protect the boundaries of dance genres and categories actually discourages change and individual expression, forcing artists to "stay in their lanes," as opposed to innovating within the form. This mode of thinking may deter dancers from creatively expanding outside of these categories if they choose to.

On the other hand, the perspective that a dance archive is a figurative receptacle for memories associated with cultural identity formation arises from a more theoretical approach to archives in dance and performance. Dance can fill in the gaps when material archives are lost or never recorded, or when written narratives are called into question. Here, we draw on performance studies scholar Diana Taylor's well-known framework of archive and repertoire to consider how performance contributes to communal memory. She describes "the repertoire" as embodied practices that substitute for missing, repressed, or corrupted "archives" so that cultural knowledge is preserved. For her, performance is a "vital act of transfer, transmitting social knowledge, memory, and a sense of identity through reiterated, or ... 'twice-behaved' behavior" (2003, 2–3). Taylor describes the shift from the archive to the repertoire as a shift from the written to the embodied and the discursive to the performative: "The live can never be contained in the archive; the archive endures beyond the limits of the live" (2003, 173)—that is, there is no definitive separation between the two. Drawing on Taylor, we conceptualize a living archive as one that is created as the community repeatedly dances and engages in a ritual of performance over generations. As Harris, Barwick, and Troy observe in relation to Indigenous communities, such practices not only point to the limits of the archive but also expand its "potentialities" for preserving and creating new cultural knowledge (2002, 7). This approach to cultural historiography resonates with both of us because it considers what performance allows people to do with their bodies as opposed to what is actually stored in an archive, providing a structure that supports constant and adaptable meaning in confluent spaces over time.

As Caribbean anthropologist Michel-Rolph Trouillot explains, there is ambiguity in historicity, or in determining not what history is but how it works: "For what history is changes with time and place or, better said, history reveals itself only through the production of specific narratives" (1995, 23–25). For this reason, ethnography contributes to historical research by filling in the voices and experiences of people who have lived and been affected by these histories but have few or no written archives. Ethnography is also appropriate for investigating collective memory, especially in performed manifestations of this memory. Drawing on Paul Connerton's *How Societies Remember*, social habits like dance are "legitimating performances" (1989, 35), and the ritualistic and formalized nature of dance enacts remembrance through its form and content. Dance reflects the bodily habits of a community and can be used to express social values and re-enact cultural memories that cannot be uttered in words. Thus, dance is more than a static object that can be stored using traditional archiving methods in academia. Dancers are especially attuned to how the body continually collects information from their surrounding environments and intersecting confluences, and so thinking about how we store and access memory in our bodies and our communities can contribute to more inclusive archival practices in academia at large.

Finally, we should also always be cautious of the capabilities of the "body" in dance, which can never be fully controlled or contained. In dance, the archive is not only about how the physical body absorbs and retains cultural knowledge in the form of movement patterns but also about how the body uses and shares that information to contribute new knowledge. This knowledge can create sustainability for a dance culture, allowing practitioners to further develop the form. The crux of our discussion here is that so-called "migrant," non-mainstream dancers like ourselves have a particular expectation and responsibility—a burden, perhaps—to maintain authenticity and tradition in our forms, which means that we always have one foot in the figurative archive. Both of us struggle to be creators of new dance ideas, while also being stewards who carry tradition on our shoulders. We often feel that we do not have the liberty of innovating freely without thinking about how our creativity might be diluting our dance cultures.

By relying on the body to archive dance, embodied material affords the carrier of such information the role of creator or owner, and, in some cases, that person joins the cultural elite of that form as a culture bearer. This can be problematic when outsiders, or even insiders, enter a cultural space via a dance form, learn the culture through dance, and then represent that culture elsewhere. In archival research about dance cultures—especially those that are non-mainstream and have not historically been represented in scholarship—we must always ask, who has created this knowledge, who owns it, and who gets to record it? And who is drawing on this knowledge to create new work? The use of provenance, provenience, and context research in the documentation of cultural knowledge production that we discuss in the following section offers a model for how scholars of traditional dance forms can engage with historical content to reproduce cultural values. This approach promotes the production of new and innovative work within (and maybe beyond) the existing structures of that cultural system that deemphasize the need for a single owner, instead ceding agency to communities to document and interpret their own dance cultures.

Provenance, provenience, and context research in dance

Provenance and provenience are common methods in art history and archaeology for understanding the function or value of an artifact or any object of historical interest. Provenience describes an object's origins up to the point of its "discovery" by collectors or researchers, whereas provenance describes the ownership journey of an object between individuals, collections, and institutions since it was found. As a result of lost or missing documentation and the constant mobility of people and objects, it is difficult and uncommon to have complete provenience or provenance of a historical object, and the journey of an object from one location to another often represents a complex history of exchange. As archaeologist James Flexner explains in the context of ethnoarchaeology, or the application of ethnographic methods to studying material culture, "the question of provenance or provenience is often associated with a need to establish the 'authenticity' of an object," as well as its history of ownership (2016, 169). In this way, collections of material culture are not only about objects themselves, but they circulate within social networks that reveal dynamics of power and agency (Byrne et al. 2011).

Museum archaeologist Alex Barker cautions against conflating provenience and provenance, pointing out that considering an object's ownership before it is found (provenience) versus after it is found (provenance) may present very different, maybe even contradictory, interpretations of an object's past. He argues that, in studies of material culture, an object's past value is always subject to inferences based on its present context (2012). This is why a third approach, context, is necessary to understand what an object was used for, or "the ways an object is and was interpreted and used within a cultural milieu" (Flexner 2016, 167). The study of context discourages the presentation of an object's history as a series of chronological landmark events, and asks: What events were not included in this object's history because they were forgotten or deemed unimportant? What are the events that seemed unremarkable at the time but critically shaped experiences with this object at that time? These unrecorded or untold contextual details are crucial for future generations whose perceived value relies on how these histories have been shaped. Context research considers networks of people and events in order to dig into the details of cultural histories surrounding an object.

Because dance cannot be classified exactly as an object or an artifact, we adapt these approaches by considering the continuity of dance as practice, identity, and exploration. Similar to our invocation of Robin Bernstein's theory of "dances with things" in Chapter 2 about the aesthetic value of non-mainstream forms, we conceive of dance as a "thing" (and not a mere object) that is imbued with meaning and tied to behavior. That is, dance is not something to be stored in a vault, but something that continually calls upon us to interact with it. While Bernstein studies the ways that material culture "scripts" actions that "manifest the repertoire of its historical moment" (2009, 89), helping us make "responsible, limited inferences about the past" (2009, 76) when archival evidence is incomplete, so too can we think about dance steps and patterns as "scripting" historical narratives. By approaching dance as a scriptive thing instead of an object in archaeological research, we seek to understand how dance interpellates specific behavior and how historical narratives emerge from these behaviors. Because dance lives in moving bodies and is not a tangible object with a traceable past, provenience and provenance research is complicated. The challenge is to identify embodied elements and patterns that help us trace the so-called "ownership" of a dance from body to body.

Our application of provenance, provenience, and context in dance takes into account (1) the body as a source; (2) culture as a channel for both transmission and retention; and (3) technologies that extend one's body knowledge beyond their immediate community. This research, of course, requires a multilayered and interdisciplinary approach that supports the creation of methodological sequences that can encapsulate the extraordinarily complicated terrain that is the study of dance in an increasingly globalized world. In dance research, films, videos, books, audio materials, and notations often become a central point of reference. But these artifacts only represent a partial snapshot, video clip, or sound bite from a dance culture's history. Not only do they fail to capture the dance as it is activated in the body, but they also fail to capture the value and significance that arises from community engagement with the dance.

Non-mainstream forms are especially underrepresented in academic archives, but we cannot assume that there is no history to tell if these materials do not exist. With modern technology, we as dance scholars have access to resources that can tell us about the origins and languages of people who dance, where they live, who their neighbors or collaborators are, and the interpersonal and intercultural interactions they have. For example, Sinclair notes how current political borders in Africa supersede pre-colonial cultural boundaries that do, in fact, still exist today, despite colonial efforts to erase them. The Akoto dance, for example, consists of distinct styles in Ghana, Togo, Benin, and Nigeria. But all these styles share a cultural history, as well as similar nomenclature, rhythms, and attitudes, all of which continue to influence each other today. Provenance and provenience prompt us to trace migrational patterns into and out of the community of origin beyond the limitations of national or political boundaries and other inflexible, colonialist frameworks. As we describe at the end of this chapter, digital technologies and data visualization software can help us catalog dance notations, visualize geo-location data, and view films and videos with the goal of better understanding communities and how they interact with a dance form over space and time.

Although time-consuming, difficult, and often messy, provenience, provenance, and context also help us incorporate stories in the archive to better understand how people have used dance to build historical narratives to describe their own origins. Context, in particular, seeks to understand what dances are used for, how they are practiced in a community, and how to develop research that benefits that community. Without understanding its context, "an object is meaningless and without value … not based on its formal or aesthetic properties, but rather on our contextualization of those properties within a time, a place, and an aesthetic tradition" (Barker 2012, 22). Relying on videos, notational scores, and other tangible archival sources that only capture a dance's formal or aesthetic properties is not sufficient for holistic and ethically responsible research, especially for dance forms that have been historically misunderstood or decontextualized.

To apply these approaches to one example, Sinclair draws a relationship between past colonial empires in Africa to their present day, as in the case of France and Francophone African countries. Makossa/Soukous is a cultural and social form that became widely popular in the early 2000s. Songs sung in native languages and French, and their accompanying dances, were developed in countries like Côte d'Ivoire, Mali, parts of Cameroon, and the Congos. These products were sold and promoted in France, often by African communities living there. We can determine the location of the dance's origins in Africa (provenience), and we can also identify the communities outside of that original location where the dances were "discovered" (provenance) by the mainstream music industry in France, where they gained even more popularity in the diaspora. Provenance and provenience not only help us trace the negative implications of cultural appropriation, but these methods also illuminate the symbiotic and reciprocal relationship between these communities, which rely on each other for their dance forms to continue to develop. Context research further prompts us to consider how artists in the French music industry, for example, may or may not provide royalties or rights to their Francophone counterparts in Africa. For example, if a Makossa music video went viral on YouTube ten years ago, context research would require us to consider who posted it, when it was posted, the demographics of the thousands of people who have seen it and reposted it, and who has placed monetary value on it. By undertaking this research, we would gather as much information as possible about the people who have elongated the dance culture's history by participating in it, either as a creator, consumer, or re-producer. We could seek out quantitative data that tell us the number of Makossa music videos produced in a particular year and location; the amount of monetary benefit that creators received from the dances' effectiveness and popularity; and the amount of monetary or reputational benefit that did or did not reach the communities of origin. In addition to the reposting of content, we could consider how future creations by other artists were directly or indirectly influenced by that work to produce new work.

Provenance and provenience research in dance largely relies on quantitative data associated with geospatial information, popularity ratings, and financial success that can be relatively easy to document in charts and timelines. However, we must also consider contextual data sources that are less straightforward in terms of our ability to analyze them. In the following section, we consider how storytelling, including gossip and rumor, plays a role in how dances become meaningful within communities. This aspect of our work with provenance, provenience, and context contributes much-needed complexity, contradiction, and nuance that makes it difficult to fully reconcile or explain the entirety of a dance culture at once, emphasizing the dynamic process of constructing an archive of dance as it moves from body to body through asymmetrical relations and exchange.

Storytelling, gossip, and rumor in dance research

Our vision of provenance research in dance necessitates including community leaders in the process of documenting their own dance cultures. One challenge with bringing such leaders into academic spaces is that their knowledge does not always take a form that is valued according to academic standards. We have both had encounters with colleagues who have questioned insider community knowledge in our research that is not backed by "primary sources" because it did not look like typical academic research or because it contradicted what was documented in a dance's written record. Are the people who live and breathe the culture not primary sources? Do they have to have an academic degree or Western certification or cite published sources to be taken seriously? Consistent references to the academic record as an unquestioned seat of knowledge make it difficult to involve communities and the complexities that they bring to a dance's cultural historiography. Our methods must be updated to reconsider what counts as a "primary source" and to build community-affirming archives that accommodate more diverse voices, indigenous methodologies, and inclusive perspectives, giving agency to community members themselves.

Oral storytelling is a central part of African dance cultures. Sinclair understands how "the talk" has been a learning modality for him at different stages of his life—not just in terms of dance, but in his cultural practices more broadly, all of which are interconnected in his experience. For him, "the talk" refers to how spiritual, temporal, and meaning-making information is transmitted from body to body through knowledge that parents pass down to their children about life, living, and community participation. For Nigerians, talking and listening while actively reacting or responding teaches one how to "be" within the community. As a child, Sinclair remembers how much of this "talk" was censored from him. When he heard his mother and aunts talk, they would ask him to go outside and not listen in. This practice of talking and gossiping formed the basis of how he learned, from a young age, to navigate his culture and community because it told him what he needed to know to adapt and be fully developed within that community. Further, in Urhobo dance, the messages embedded within "the talk" are lyrically and rhythmically present in the music and ululations. These messages often guide the performance and tell people how to behave. For example, a stylistic and flamboyant display occurs as a caller cries, "Do do do do, Urhobo, Mini Wado," and receives the response, "Eh"—all of which is repeated and modulated 3–4 times, signaling the call to dance and be present and receptive to new information during the performance. This connection between "the talk" and a dance's processes and modalities exemplifies how culturally defined networks of communication are vital in dance research.

Part of the "messiness" of historical research arises from the stories that we tell ourselves and that we tell each other—sometimes in the form of gossip and rumor. Storytelling and gossip are central to our view of provenance, provenience, and context research in dance because these forms of communication reveal local values and perspectives. Historian Luise White notes in her study of vampire stories in colonial Africa that "people do not speak with the truth, with a concept of the accurate description of what they saw, to say what they mean, but they construct and repeat stories that carry the values and meanings that most forcibly get their points across" (2000, 30). In this way, historical truth is continually negotiated and even contradicted, and "the confusions and the misunderstandings [that arise] show what is important [to a community]" (2000, 43). White uses this approach to oral history, based on over 130 interviews with colonial subjects in East and Central African societies, in conjunction with written sources to construct a narrative that relies on their own words, not hers. Much of this narrative is predicated on gossip, rumor, and even silence as reliable sources of information. Importantly, she does not draw a clear line between primary and secondary sources, highlighting that what historians consider factual evidence has always, in fact, been interpreted by some intermediary.

We believe that gossip and rumor are useful in provenance research about dance because this form of communication provides the opportunity for multilayered interpretation that accounts for the value of local knowledge. Although complicated and difficult to trace, incorporating hearsay into archival research allows for the interweaving of multiple voices and bodies in the creation of historical narratives, rather than privileging and preserving the voice of one authoritative creator or owner. Gossip and rumor reinforce embodied knowledge across spatial and temporal borders, helping a community generate new, adaptable frameworks for understanding their own history and cultural practices, even after being repeated thousands of times. Dance, as a non-verbal embodied form, is like a game of telephone that may or may not maintain some semblance of the original, but still remains connected to that origin. Historical constructions of dance forms are built on a foundation of both what people say and what they do with their bodies, even if what they say and do are at odds with one another. This process restores agency to communities of origin and allows individual practitioners to contribute to histories in decentralized ways, which is especially important for dance cultures that have been subjected to colonial silencing, censorship, and repression. In addition, accepting rumor and gossip into the archival record of a dance form establishes that provenance and provenience are less about proving the historical accuracy of a story and more about leaning into debates, contradictions, and anxieties to better understand how community values adapt as dances pass from body to body.

In Kate's studies of masquerades on Montserrat in 2013–2016, for instance, she relied heavily on often-contradictory stories about the island's cultural heritage told by different community members. This was confusing and disorienting for an outsider like herself. Although she felt compelled to locate written documents searching for the truth, she realized that even if such documents existed, they often provided less insight into the dance culture than what various individuals told her—many of whom disagreed with each other and maintained that their version of the information was correct. To take the example of the heel and toe polka described in the previous chapter, local community leaders referred to it as the "Irish" step in their masquerade tradition, tracing its roots back to a slave rebellion planned for St. Patrick's Day in 1768. According to the island's popular narrative, enslaved Africans performed the heel and toe polka as a mockery of Irish masters dancing and drinking during the holiday's festivities. However, the practice of a so-called "heel and toe polka" is not supported by documentation of traditional dance in Ireland during that era, and the "polka" was not even referred to as such until the nineteenth century in Central Europe (Zíbrt 1895). Thus, the idea that the heel and toe polka dates back to around 1768 is not supported by the historical record. But the historical plausibility of this story is beside the point. Contradictory perspectives about the Irishness of Montserrat's masquerades arising from conversations, stories, and debates that take place around St. Patrick's Day each year reveal a certain ambivalence about the island's Irish heritage, as something to be celebrated for its uniqueness (and potential for the tourism economy) and/or resisted for its association with White, European culture. If we consider the masquerade dance's cultural transformations from its origins in both African and Irish dance forms and its trajectory through different bodies from Ireland and West Africa to Montserrat, we come to better understand how dances and cultural practices are shaped by the conversations that Montserratians have about their history and cultural identity.

Debates about Irish and African retentions in Montserratian cultural practices like the masquerades have produced debates and anxieties among some scholars researching the island's past about cultural mythologies that are not backed by historical evidence or primary sources (Messenger 1967, 1994; Fergus 1981; Akenson 1997). Kate's research, however, focused on the specific role of dance and performance in identity formation, through which invented traditions and cultural myths are just as relevant as (if not more relevant than) what is considered historically accurate according to traditional archival sources (Spanos 2017, 2019). During her fieldwork, all of this information was, of course, filtered through her own eyes, ears, and body as an outsider, and she sought to center the voices of community members in her writing. This involved embracing the ways that narratives were often conflicted and highly contested, as well as resisting the urge to try to reconcile contradictions and neatly tie up the research with a bow, as though to legitimize the research with an authoritative argument. The desire to reconcile contradictions is tied to the overarching Western system of logic, which touts the prevailing notion that something or someone has to be correct. As anthropologists Kurzwelly, Rapport, and Spiegel note, "Appreciation of contradiction leads to a modelling of human social life not as something coherent but rather as a muddling through" (2020, 76). Debates themselves often arise from the sense that a community must prove the value of the dance or cultural practice. The more threatened a dance community is, the more individuals will debate its meaning and try to establish ownership and authority. Leaving interpretations open and revealing their complexities takes the focus off of the individual researcher as a creator of history and places this agency into the hands of the community who continue to build their own interpretations of that history. Thus, provenance research requires listening to what people say about their dances as a living archive in connection with what their bodies do when they dance, establishing a taxonomy that prioritizes insider community knowledge and takes into account when people tell different stories, disagree about what a story means, or even take the opportunity to adapt stories to serve their own agendas.

In a related example of African and Irish cultural encounters in the United States, American tap dance is one dance form with a contested history that arises not only from oral storytelling but also from rumored embodied citations of past and present dancers. We can theorize about the development of tap through the borrowings, (mis)interpretations, and appropriations of rhythms and movements in the United States since the 1800s. Tap history is filled with examples of dancers taking ownership of steps, naming themselves the original creators of a move- ment, and borrowing (or stealing) from others to make their mark in the form's embodied archive. The way that American percussive forms like tap and Appala- chian flatfooting and clogging developed among African, Irish and Scots Irish, and Indigenous communities living in close proximity in urban centers and rural areas, respectively, points to how embodied knowledge hops from dancer to dancer and is nearly impossible to trace (Hill 2010; Jamison 2015). This rhizomatic spread of influences continues among percussive dancers today. The auditory nature of per- cussive dance also lends itself to comparisons to conversation and dialogue. Tap historian Constance Valis Hill draws on Thomas Talley's quote that "the feet beat a tattoo upon the ground, answering to every word, and sometimes to every syl- lable of the rhyme" (1922, 296–297, qtd. in Hill 2010, 17). This idea calls to mind the "signifyin'" of Henry Louis Gates, Jr., based on African American vernacular practices in writing and culture (1988), such that rhythmic footwork produces a dialogue that "echoes" and "signifies" the calls and responses of dancers through- out history. These sounds, in turn, tattoo the figurative ground in a kind of archival documentation of the process. As an Irish dancer, Kate is particularly interested in the ways that dancers in her community incorporate tap motifs and syncopations into Irish dancing, not only because of the obvious technical affinities between these two percussive forms but also in response to the explicit and implicit histori- cal connections between them. Narratives reinforce these connections and prompt collaborations that perpetuate a cycle of cross-pollination across communities. The interplay between dancers over generations within one genre and across similar genres can be both seen and heard in the footwork itself.

Incorporating gossip and rumor into our approaches to provenance, provenience, and context allows us to trace community values more deeply. When researching dance, gossip is not only what is said about the dance, but it also encompasses the responses and "riffings off" of other dancers that we produce in embodied ways. Taking these forms of communication into account in academic research can serve as a catalyst to produce knowledge within a community and, crucially, for the reproduction of knowledge. Acknowledging local communication networks helps us understand how structures of dance performance relate to Taylor's notion of repetition, reiteration, and twice-behaved behavior (2003). It also helps us better understand how traditional artists who engage with generations-old material are not "just" copying each other's steps (see Chapter 4) but contributing to cultural continuity and communal memory-making. Whether an artist or a scholar is engaging with a dance form, one must understand the product in order to reproduce cultural knowledge and, potentially, produce something new.

Technology and ethnography in future research

The arguments that we have made throughout this book about how to navigate confluent spaces, value non-mainstream dance cultures, and give back to communities require highly sophisticated, decentralized, non-authoritative networks. We believe that such networks can be supported by technologies and algorithms from the field of digital humanities that would provide agency to dance communities all over the world to share their cultures on their own terms. Many of the institutional databases that currently exist are not ideal because they tend to be inaccessible to most, often protected by steep paywalls. We envision taking advantage of open-source, crowdsourced platforms on which we could store and share information and contribute to community archives.[2] Throughout this book, we have discussed challenging the categorization that is used to classify different dance forms. New technologies can provide an opportunity to build flexibility and versatility into archival systems. We should have systems designed to handle and adapt to inevitable changes in preferred nomenclature, terminologies, and categories in our field, as well as to integrate with other systems as technology develops. This approach allows us to digitally trace footprints of dance practices within and across cultures, visualize geospatial and lineage data, and hold up the complexities that arise from community-built narratives. In addition, simply publishing content is not enough. We must be intentional about how we participate in shared intellectual engagements with communities. Most importantly, we need technologies that trace origins to protect property in more equitable ways and to give credit and remuneration where it is due.

As scholars, we are interested in how provenance, provenience, and context can help us conceive of how to use digital technologies to store information in online open-access hubs. These hubs would include a combination of filmed dances, interactive maps, location data, human migration data, family trees or kinship diagrams, value aesthetics, oral histories and interviews, and notational scores. We think about open access in terms of offering the ability for communities to engage with information without the financial, logistical, and educational barriers that many academic institutions put up. This access relates to the legibility we discussed in Chapter 1, trading in academic language and coding with emic ter-minology, cultural codes, and aesthetic value systems. Our communities already produce and archive dance-related material online, but they are scattershot across cultural, sociopolitical, and academic borders, making them hard to organize, as-sess, and make use of. We are aware of concerns that fully open-access platforms would be difficult to curate and control, but we also feel confident that insiders would be able to determine what is valuable and useful to the community or not, and there is room for contradictions and disagreements around questions of authen-ticity that point to what insiders care about. Central to our vision of open access is ensuring that dance communities know that such platforms exist and that they are intended for their use.

From the data sources stored on these platforms, we could also build visualiza-tions to trace historical and migrational patterns in a dance form's development,[3] and innovations in motion-capture and 3D technologies can also contribute com-plex data sets to examine movement patterns and aesthetics within and across dance cultures.[4] This is not a top-down approach to curating culture, but it is a method that would enable us to visualize what is already going on in the com-munity, to examine where a dance form comes from, where it is most often found, who practices it, and who is committed to the continuity and sustainability of the form. New methods are being developed to give us the broad swath of information required to conduct the deep multivariable analyses that we need to make intracul-tural and intercultural connections within and across dance forms. We see this as especially useful in teaching and research as we guide students and researchers to more clearly see the dynamic confluences that shape a specific dance culture. For example, in this multivariate framework, a person researching one African dance form would understand that the form does not exist in a vacuum but is part of a larger constellation of dance communities that interact and influence each other. This type of platform would promote collaboration, community input, and cross-cultural information sharing among dance cultures worldwide.

At the time of writing this book, both of us are working on our own separate projects that draw on the framework of cultural confluences that we present here. We are both interested in harnessing technologies to collate and present informa-tion about how our communities produce and reproduce materials that promote a fuller understanding of historical and contemporary practices and knowledge of the dance cultures we study. In building digital networks to identify and trace rela-tionships between movement forms in confluent spaces, our projects examine the migrations of people and their dances.[5]

Sinclair is developing "Living Archive: Analysis, Description, and Assem-blages," a project that arises from his interest in synthesizing multilayered accounts to promote and legitimize dances of African peoples around the world. The project addresses the challenges of information loss and cultural extinction that arise from the legacies of colonialism, slavery, and other forms of oppression and displace-ment that have affected Africans. His team applies multi-variant frameworks of the-oretical inquiry such as geospatial archeological methods, geoarchaeology, remote sensing, systematic survey, and settlement change. Systematic survey methods allow him to gather data on the general presence or absence of dance materials in the archive, as well as define resource types or estimate the distribution, usages, and re-creation of dance materials within world knowledge banks. However, the complexity of Africa's geography and human history requires a system that can address the vast array of cultural specificity within African communities and the migration of these communities across space and time. Remote sensing methods (used to observe an object or place from a distance, as in NASA's observations of Earth through satellites and aircraft) allow him to understand a geographical area and changes in terrain over time. He can access these data through simulations to gather information about human migration and settlement, and then connect the data to patterns of cross-cultural dance pollination in various parts of Africa.

He applies provenance, provenience, and context approaches, along with ethnographic methodologies, to analyze dance origins through cultural narratives and embodied analysis across cultural and spatial boundaries. As noted in the last section, African cultural and performing arts rely on storytelling, including gossip and rumor, or what would be referred to by Western scholars as "oral tradition." The embodied practices of dance in Africa take root in the transference of body knowledge through sophisticated means based on linguistics, stories, religions, and cross-cultural pollination of attitudes and dramatic narratives among surrounding settlements. Based on this assessment, in order to understand the dances of African communities, one has to understand their linguistic practices as much as their geographical locales. Sinclair's position as a recent immigrant to the United States from Nigeria affords him the privilege of embodying his culture as an African, and also cast the diasporic eye of a distant migrant African, allowing him to develop research methodologies that will expand and more intricately survey the complexities of understanding African dance cultures.

"Living Archive" takes advantage of technological advances to promote cross-cultural and community contributions, collaborations, and disseminations. This interactive platform will not only provide a repository for African dance collections, but it will also be a place where members of the community can upload their own creations, which will represent local knowledge and intellectuality from local cultures. Overlays on maps of the African continent will show ancestral, cultural, and ethnic ties between peoples and associate these data with videos and narratives crowdsourced from Africans based on geographic and cultural criteria. Privileging community knowledge in the description of videos will remove the colonial lens and could reveal novel insights. In moving community knowledge from the margins of academic inquiry to the center, the project breaks down traditional academic hierarchies that privilege the outside observer's worldview over an insider's own knowledge and beliefs.

Ultimately, Sinclair envisions "Living Archive" to be a resource to trace dance origins for African people and diasporic communities across the world, facilitating more robust scholarly discourse on African dances. In a time when the field of dance is engaged in many conversations about diversity, equity, inclusion, and representation, there is a need for theoretical frameworks that allow African performance to be taken seriously as worthy of study through critical lenses. Immersive frameworks arising from the ideas presented in this book provide more than a one-off studio-based dance class, emphasizing a more holistic approach to the study of the presence of African dance in our global academy of dance research and performance.

In the realm of Irish dance, Kate is also developing an archival project that involves technology and ethnographic storytelling. In 2018, she built an archival database prototype[6] to organize over 300 steps from her 30 years of Irish dancing, which she had documented in videos and notations on various hard drives and in old notebooks over the years. The impetus came from the realization that her body had learned and accumulated much cultural information over the years, all of which, when taken together, felt valuable. Weighed down by the burden of feeling like a physical archive of steps with a responsibility to remember them, she became concerned about forgetting or losing the neural patterns encoded in her body as she ages. She organized everything into a searchable and taggable relational database with videos, notations, and metadata, including tags for categorizing styles and rhythmic families (jigs, reels, slip jigs, hornpipes, etc.), relatives within family trees between steps associated by teacher or group, and, importantly, stories and memories that provide context about where she learned them, from whom, and any anecdotes she associated with a particular step.

In the future, she wants to license the software for individual use, as well as expand the project to take on a Wiki format for crowdsourcing so that community members can contribute dance materials and annotations to an open-access archive. A shared database could contribute to broader investigations about how embodied knowledge and aesthetic value in the Irish dance community are transmitted through a combination of the physical body and archival video. Kate is working with collaborators Rebecca McGowan and Samantha Jones on a project titled "Cartlann: Dancing the Archive" (*cartlann* means "archive" in Irish) to reconstruct Irish dance repertoire from videos posted online that were recorded in Ireland and the United States from the 1950s through the 1990s, reflecting a period preceding Riverdance, the show that brought about radical changes to the form. This reconstruction process is a sort of archaeological dig—dusting off steps, putting the pieces together (especially when steps have been cut off by camera angles and video editing), and using them to make sense of past Irish dance culture. The reconstruction of steps as "artifacts" involves piecing together an introspective analysis of rhythms, motifs, and styles in comparison to one's bodily habits, seeking to understand how they were composed and performed in their historical and cultural contexts compared to today. The process also involves oral history interviews with dancers featured in the archival videos—men and women now in their 60s, 70s, and 80s—to understand where and how they learned particular steps and how they approached choreography and performance at the time of recording. This study offers a window into past styles that have been forgotten and were not transmitted to younger generations as a result of the popularization, commercialization, and globalization of Irish dance competition and spectacularized show styles.[7,8] Using such community-driven, collaborative database technologies to document, organize, and visualize these data, this work offers a multidimensional framework for thinking about how these steps carry cultural meaning through the Irish dance diaspora that goes beyond simply recording or notating steps as though they are static objects.

When the two of us first started writing this book, we were unsure how we fit into academia or what we could contribute. We see the potential for technology to help us create a sort of "road map" to visualize and describe the cultural migrations within confluent spaces that we have experienced as dancers. Technological developments increasingly offer the ability to handle the complex variability, relationships, permeability, and multidimensionality that we need to more fully describe movement and adaptation in the dance cultures we study. Working with technology also opens up opportunities to collaborate with other fields like software engineering, information sciences, and archaeology. It can also help make space for the voices of individuals and communities from outside of academia. By applying and further developing the technologies described above to our projects, we can more clearly see where we are in the dance field and how we can move forward.

Conclusion

We have written this book because, although many scholars and artists have made many of the same points through their studies of individual dance cultures, we believe that we need to consider how the dance field at large can be more inclusive and equitable in its treatment of these cultures. This cannot happen without looking at patterns and connections between seemingly disparate dance cultures—like Nigerian and Irish dance, for example—and understanding why dancers struggle for equity and representation in mainstream academia in their own ways. While we have repeatedly expressed throughout this book our feelings of being "nowhere" in the dance field, stuck between impermeable streams of categories, brands, and identity markers that do not fully account for our experiences, the notion of confluences allows us to feel like we have "somewhere" in which to place ourselves and make sense of those experiences. The practice of studying individual dances separately is often justified by the idea that studying complex societies, culturally dense communities, and highly codified practices independently achieves a more holistic understanding of the form itself. There is much to be gained from this approach. However, we are concerned that the effects of studying non-mainstream dances through mainstream academic frameworks, language, and methodologies also inflict harm on these cultures that outweigh positive intentions to further their preservation. Western scholarship—which includes Western and non-Western scholars using Western frameworks and methodologies—tends to devalue community knowledge and pulls cultures apart in order to study them under a microscope, pitting them against each other and promoting specific groups as more advanced simply because there is more written about them. This is not to say that Western scholarship is inherently bad, but we must consider other approaches to diversify how we look at dance. Staying with one system for too long hinders the development of any type of research.

The greatest challenge we have had while writing this book has been writing about dance within an academic context while arguing (1) that the full extent of dance expression cannot be documented in writing, and (2) that our studies of dance should extend beyond Western academia and challenge the very structures that we, as practitioners and scholars, currently navigate and write for. Writing offers a sense of "control" over a topic, and the need for control is especially tempting when writing about a topic as complex, multilayered, and uncontrollable as bodies, especially dancing bodies. Still, we have argued throughout this book that dance is bigger than what can be expressed verbally. Why does academia make us feel like dance is limited by being difficult to write about when it is actually the written word that is limited? The issue is not how we can better fit dance into written scholarship, but instead how written scholarship comprises just one aspect of dance research. We can adapt new language for the ways we talk about dance to convey a broader diversity of motivations and values for dancers around the world. In writing about dance, something is always left unexpressed—how it feels to dance, what the dancing body just "knows," and how dance makes us feel like we are part of something larger than ourselves. We should encourage people to move, dance, listen, and respond with their full bodies.

The questions we have raised throughout this book are especially important for what we have referred to as non-mainstream dance forms. The pervasive idea that scholars cannot convey adequate intellectual knowledge of these forms because of an apparent lack of scholarship or institutional documentation diminishes their value, as well as the value of those who practice them. In many communal dance forms, "the body is everything," as we stated in Chapter 2. Throughout this book, we have identified some of the issues that both of us see and have experienced as practitioners of forms that are non-mainstream where we live in the United States, and we have offered our vision for creating new frameworks within academia that can support the research and practice of these forms. Current frameworks limit us and colonize us—all of us.

Academia also demands that we, as scholars, put an authoritative stamp on our work when we publish books and articles so that we can add them to our curricula vitae and call ourselves experts. However, both of us believe that dance scholarship should never be about a single author or a single creator. Instead, it should always lean into the complexity of many voices and many bodies. As academics, we should feel comfortable ceding control to communities of origin when talking about their dance practices. Our process of co-writing this book has taught us many lessons about how dancers from very different backgrounds, like ourselves, can dialogue about their practices in ways that build on each other's ideas but also allow for disagreement and debate. Neither one of us has been able to take authority as the single creator of this work and we have gently challenged each other to think about these issues in different ways. We have intentionally kept some of our disagreements in our writing because editing them out would remove the fraught discourse and exchange of ideas that are central to the process that we advocate for. In our conversations and collaborative writing, we have both had many moments of vulnerability, insecurity, and self-doubt, as well as moments of confidence and conviction—feelings that often arise directly from our cultural upbringings and racialized experiences.

To lay the groundwork for our vision for change in the dance field, we have analyzed how language shapes the dance field and plays a part in how our field values some forms more than others. We have discussed the challenges that migratory dancers experience when translating and transposing their aesthetic values and creative processes to new spaces, and we have framed these spaces as confluent meeting points for many cultural perspectives. Finally, we have questioned what it means to archive dance and produce (and reproduce) cultural knowledge through the body. The field of dance at large would benefit from a shift in perspective that takes into account the ways that, in today's globalized world, all dancers are in a constant state of confluence with other dancers. Dance cannot be contained, and we should not try to contain it.

Notes

1 Catherine E. Foley expands on the notion of collecting steps, and the "fear of losing a step," in traditional Irish step dance in her book, *Step Dancing in Ireland: Culture and History* (2013, 93–130).

2 Some notably innovative projects that use technological advances for dance archiving include: (1) Gesel Mason's "No Boundaries," which, according to her website, was initiated in 2004 as a "part archival database and part community engagement" for work by Black choreographers that allows "participation formats for user-generated content so that users can contribute, communicate, share, and learn"; see https://www.geselmason.com/no-boundaries; (2) historian and computer engineer Ademide Adelusi-Adeluyi's "New Maps of Old Lagos," which compares contemporary maps to historical plans in order to document the Nigerian capital's public history. Sinclair notes that these visualizations show borders that have created prescribed identities of the people living there—identities which appear in cultural dance practices; see https://newmapsoldlagos.com; and (3) "Enslaved: Peoples of the Historical Slave Trade," an open-source database created by Walter Hawthorne, Dean Rehberger, and Daryle Williams to "discover, connect, and visualize" the stories of enslaved peoples through archival fragments and detailed datasets gathered from people, sources, and events; see http://enslaved.org.

3 The project, "Dunham's Data: Katherine Dunham and Digital Methods for Dance Historical Inquiry," directed by Kate Elswit and Harmony Bench, is one model for providing migrational data visualizations in dance through the work of Katherine Dunham as an individual choreographer. The project's interactive maps and charts present various angles on the complexity of "how movement moves," and it would be interesting to see this approach expanded beyond one individual's work to look at a dance culture more broadly. See https://www.dunhamsdata.org/.

4 For examples of motion-capture for comparative movement studies and cultural heritage preservation, see Iyengar et al.'s study to create an open repository of comparative movement (2016) and the WhoLoDancE project (http://www.wholodance.eu).

5 In 2014–2016, both of us were involved in "Re-imaging and Re-imagining Choreometrics," a project led by dance researcher Karen Bradley at the University of Maryland and anthropologist Anna Lomax Wood, then-president and executive director of the Association of Cultural Equity. The project examined new technologies to reimagine Alan Lomax's Choreometrics collection of films captured from dance communities around the world in the 1930s and 1940s. Our involvement in this project provided both of us with insights into the application of technology to archival dance research.

6 Kate's dance database prototype was built with a MySQL and a Javascript/jQuery-powered browser interface.

7 "Our Steps, Our Story: An Irish Dance Legacy Archive," created and directed by Irish dancer, choreographer, and scholar Jean Butler in 2018, is a project with a similar goal to document steps of the past through archival residencies based around live intergenerational transmission of steps, as well as oral histories with dancers who grew up dancing

in the mid-twentieth century in Ireland and the United States. See https://www.our-steps.com.

8 See also the use of "postcolonial agency" and "proactive archiving" in the National Dance Archive of Ireland, housed at the University of Limerick (Foley 2016).

References

Ajayi-Soyinka, Omofolabo. 1998. *Yoruba Dance: The Semiotics of Movement and Body Attitude in a Nigerian Culture.* Trenton, NJ: Africa World Press.

Akenson, Donald Harman. 1997. *If the Irish Ran the World: Montserrat, 1630–1730.* Montreal, Québec: McGill-Queen's University Press.

Ballard, Chris. 2014. "Oceanic Historicities." *The Contemporary Pacific* 26 (1): 96–124. https://doi.org/10.1353/cp.2014.0009.

Barker, Alex. 2012. "Provenience, Provenance and Context(s)." In *The Futures of Our Pasts: Ethical Implications of Collecting Antiquities in the Twenty-First Century*, edited by Michael A. Adler and Susan Benton Bruning, 19–30. Santa Fe, NM: School for Advanced Research Press.

Barrett, Estelle, and Barbara Bolt. 2007. *Practice as Research: Approaches to Creative Arts Enquiry.* London, UK: I.B. Tauris.

Bernstein, Robin. 2009. "Dances with Things: Material Culture and the Performance of Race." *Social Text* 101: 67–94.

Boast, Robin. 2011. "Neocolonial Collaboration: Museum as Contact Zone Revisited." *Museum Anthropology* 34 (1): 56–70. https://doi.org/10.1111/j.1548-1379.2010.01107.x.

Byrne, Sarah, Anne Clarke, Rodney Harrison, and Robin Torrence, eds. 2011. *Unpacking the Collection: Networks of Material and Social Agency in the Museum.* New York, NY: Springer New York. https://doi.org/10.1007/978-1-4419-8222-3.

Chernoff, John Miller. 1979. *African Rhythm and African Sensibility: Aesthetics and Social Action in African Musical Idioms.* Chicago, IL: University of Chicago Press.

Clifford, James. 1997. *Routes: Travel and Translation in the Late Twentieth Century.* Cambridge, MA: Harvard University Press.

Connerton, Paul. 1989. *How Societies Remember.* Cambridge, UK: Cambridge University Press.

Derrida, Jacques, and Eric Prenowitz. 1996. *Archive Fever: A Freudian Impression.* Religion and Postmodernism. Chicago, IL: University of Chicago Press.

"Documenting Dance: A Practical Guide." 2006. Dance Heritage Coalition, Inc.

Douglas, Jennifer. 2018. "A Call to Rethink Archival Creation: Exploring Types of Creation in Personal Archives."*Archival Science* 18 (1): 29–49. https://doi.org/10.1007/s10502-018-9285-8.

Enekwe, Ossie Onuora. 1991. *Theories of Dance in Nigeria: An Introduction.* Nsukka: Afa Press.

Fergus, Howard. 1981. "Montserrat 'Colony of Ireland': The Myth and the Reality." *Studies* 70: 325–40.

Flexner, James L. 2016. "Archaeology and Ethnographic Collections: Disentangling Provenance, Provenience, and Context in Vanuatu Assemblages." *Museum Worlds* 4 (1): 167–80. https://doi.org/10.3167/armw.2016.040113.

Foley, Catherine E. 2013. *Step Dancing in Ireland: Culture and History.* Burlington, VT: Ashgate.

———. 2016. "Postcolonial Agency, Proactive Archiving, and Applied Ethnochoreology: The National Dance Archive of Ireland." *Český Lid* 103 (4): 623–34.

Foster, Susan Leigh. 2019. *Valuing Dance: Commodities and Gifts in Motion*. New York, NY: Oxford University Press. https://doi.org/10.1093/oso/9780190933975.001.0001.

Gates, Henry Louis, Jr. 1988. *The Signifying Monkey: A Theory of African-American Literary Criticism*. Oxford, UK: Oxford University Press.

Gore, Georgiana. 1999. "Textual Fields: Representation in Dance Ethnography." In *Dance in the Field: Theory, Methods and Issues in Dance Ethnography*, edited by Teresa J. Buckland, 208–20. New York, NY: St. Martin's Press.

Harris, Amanda, Linda Barwick, and Jakelin Troy, eds. 2002. *Music, Dance and the Archive*. Sydney: Sydney University Press.

Hill, Constance Valis. 2010. *Tap Dancing America: A Cultural History*. Oxford, UK: Oxford University Press.

Iyengar, Varsha, Grisha Coleman, David Tinapple, and Pavan Turaga. 2016. "Motion, Captured: An Open Repository for Comparative Movement Studies." *Proceedings of the 3rd International Symposium on Movement and Computing*. https://doi.org/10.1145/2948910.2948938.

Jamison, Phil. 2015. *Hoedowns, Reels, and Frolics: Roots and Branches of Southern Appalachian Dance*. Music in American Life. Urbana, IL: University of Illinois Press.

Kurzwelly, Jonatan, Nigel Rapport, and Andrew Spiegel. 2020. "Encountering, Explaining and Refuting Essentialism." *Anthropology Southern Africa* 43 (April): 65–81. https://doi.org/10.1080/23323256.2020.1780141.

Madison, D. Soyini. 2020. *Critical Ethnography: Method, Ethics, and Performance*. Third edition. Thousand Oaks, CA: SAGE Publications.

Messenger, John C. 1967. "The Influence of the Irish in Montserrat." *Caribbean Quarterly* 13: 3–26.

———. 1994. "St. Patrick's Day in 'The Other Emerald Isle.'" *Éire-Ireland* 29: 12–23.

Phelan, Helen, and Graham F. Welch. 2021. *The Artist and Academia*. London, UK: Routledge.

Smith, Hazel, and R. T. Dean. 2009. *Practice-Led Research, Research-Led Practice in the Creative Arts*. Edinburgh: Edinburgh University Press.

Spanos, Kathleen A. 2017. "Dancing the Archive: Rhythms of Change in Montserrat's Masquerades." *Yearbook for Traditional Music* 49: 67–91. https://doi.org/10.5921/yeartradmusi.49.2017.0067.

———. 2019. "Locating Montserrat Between the Black and Green." *Irish Migration Studies in Latin America* 9 (2): 1–14.

Talley, Thomas Washington. 1922. *Negro Folk Rhymes: Wise and Otherwise*. New York, NY: Macmillan.

Taylor, Diana. 2003. *The Archive and the Repertoire: Performing Cultural Memory in the Americas*. Durham, NC: Duke University Press.

Trouillot, Michel-Rolph. 1995. *Silencing the Past: Power and the Production of History*. Boston, MA: Beacon Press.

White, Luise. 2000. *Speaking with Vampires: Rumor and History in Colonial Africa*. Studies on the History of Society and Culture. Berkeley, CA: University of California Press.

Zíbrt, Čeněk. 1895. *Jak Se Kdy v Čechách Tancovalo: Dějiny Tance v Čechách, Na Moravě, ve Slezsku a Na Slovensku z Věků Nejstarších Až Do Nové Doby Se Zvláštním Zřetelem k Dějinám Tance Vůbec*. Knihtiskárna F. Šimáček nakl.

Index